Blue Ribbon USA

Prizewinning Recipes from State and County Fairs

4-H CLUBS
THE BROWN COUNTY FAIR

FLASH HAT
PAT. NO 20 PEN.
SDPT.SPEC.B.
LEXINGTON KY   FLAGS OF NATIONS

Printed in U.S.A.

by GEORGIA ORCUTT
and JOHN MARGOLIES

CHRONICLE BOOKS
SAN FRANCISCO

Library of Congress Cataloging-in-Publication Data available.

ISBN-10: 0-8118-5484-1
ISBN-13: 978-0-8118-5484-9

Manufactured in China.

Designed by Margo Mooney

Distributed in Canada by Raincoast Books
9050 Shaughnessy Street
Vancouver, British Columbia V6P 6E5

10 9 8 7 6 5 4 3 2 1

Chronicle Books LLC
680 Second Street
San Francisco, California 94107

www.chroniclebooks.com

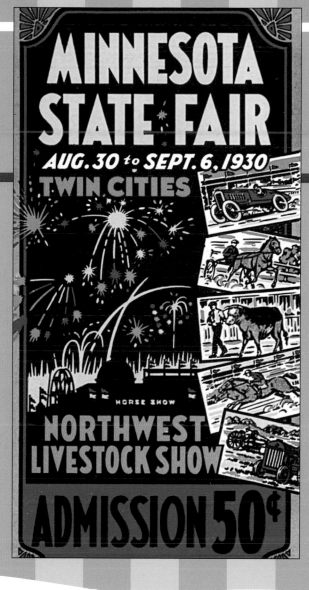

DEDICATION

To Stephen, Eli, and Amos, who eagerly
tasted all the prizewinning recipes.

—*Georgia Orcutt*

ACKNOWLEDGMENTS

We'd like to thank the following people for
their generous help in making this book
happen: Margo Mooney, for her energy,
enthusiasm, and talent; Amy Treadwell, Doug
Ogan, Evan Hulka, Steve Kim, and Ayako
Akazawa at Chronicle Books, for believing in
this idea and watching over it at every stage
of production; our agents, Jim Fitzgerald and
Wendy Burton Brouws, for their continued
support; Lew Baer, Nicholas Follansbee,
Art Groten, Helen Howard, and Alan
Rosenberg at the Triangle Poster Company,
Pittsburgh, Pennsylvania, Hal Ottaway,
and Leland and Crystal Payton, for making
images available for use in this book.

CONTENTS

Introduction 6

ALABAMA 12
Mary's Sticky Biscuits

ALASKA 14
Melody's Molasses Crinkles

ARIZONA 16
Citrus Cowboy Creams

ARKANSAS 18
Jackpot Cherry Pie

CALIFORNIA 20
Salsa Jam

COLORADO 22
Colorado Potato Cream Pie

CONNECTICUT 24
Country Fair "Caramel Apples"

DELAWARE 26
Lakeshore Italian Steak and
Potato Salad

FLORIDA 28
Pecan Fudge Caramel Squares

GEORGIA 30
Marie Antoinettes

HAWAII 32
Blue Hawaiian

IDAHO 34
Sourdough Bread

ILLINOIS 36
Soy Velvet Crumb Cake

INDIANA 38
Double-Chocolate Peanut
Butter Chip Cookies

IOWA 40
Cool Fruit Strata

KANSAS 42
Strawberry Daisy Bread

KENTUCKY 44
Aunt Betsy's Bourbon Chowder
with Onion-Pita Rounds

LOUISIANA 46
Pickled Okra

MAINE 48
New York–Style
Half-Sour Pickles

MARYLAND 50
Squash Pie

MASSACHUSETTS 52
Mini Raspberry Truffle Cakes

MICHIGAN 54
Pasties

MINNESOTA 58
Marjorie Johnson's Sour Cream
Streusel Coffee Cake

MISSISSIPPI 60
Cajun Smothered Venison Steak

MISSOURI 62
Catfish Wraps

MONTANA   66
Beef Roll-Ups

NEBRASKA   68
Creamy Cheesecake

NEVADA   70
Grilled Salsa

NEW HAMPSHIRE   72
Rosy Spiced Crab Apples

NEW JERSEY   74
Apple-Carrot Muffins

NEW MEXICO   76
Korean Oven-Roasted
Turkey SPAM Stir-Fry

NEW YORK   78
Governor Davis Apple Pie

NORTH CAROLINA   82
Roasted Chicken Salad
with Honey-Pecan
Balsamic Dressing

NORTH DAKOTA   84
Susan's Fettuccine

OHIO   86
Don's Peach Pie

OKLAHOMA   88
Oklahoma Wagon Wheels

OREGON   90
Bacon Cheeseburger
Potato Salad

PENNSYLVANIA   92
Jim Bob's
Chocolate-Molasses Cake

RHODE ISLAND   94
Apple-Cinnamon Oatmeal Bread

SOUTH CAROLINA   96
Japanese Fruitcake

SOUTH DAKOTA   98
Pumpkin Streusel Sweet Rolls

TENNESSEE   100
Strawberry Cobbler

TEXAS   102
Mushroom Moussaka

UTAH   106
Five-Minute Crock-Pot Burritos

VERMONT   108
Vegetarian Stuffed-Pepper Medley

VIRGINIA   110
Championship Chili

WASHINGTON   112
Chocolate Crunch Brownies

WEST VIRGINIA   114
Marbled Banana Bars

WISCONSIN   116
Old-Fashioned Sausages
and Peppers

WYOMING   120
Coffee Cheesecake Pie with
Coffee-Caramel Sauce

How to Win a Blue Ribbon   122
Recipe Permissions   124
Illustration Credits   125
Index   127
Table of Equivalents   128

INTRODUCTION

All roads lead to the fair. So grab your hat and come along as we travel throughout the United States to visit great American fairs and sample memorable recipes from each of the United States. We guarantee you'll have fun and take home memories that will last a lifetime: the smell and taste of fried dough and corn dogs; the thrill of riding on the Ferris wheel; the challenge of banging a wooden mallet hard enough to win a giant teddy bear; the warm sweet-and-sour air of the animal barns; the shiny blue ribbons; the sparkling jars of jams and jellies; and the expectation in the damp night air.

For more than 150 years, state and county fairs have brought people together to have a good time. The first fairs, organized in the early nineteenth century by agricultural associations, had the serious intent of giving farmers a venue for sharing information and buying and selling livestock. But county fairs also presented the opportunity to get away from the farm, to socialize, and to celebrate. Early promoters, eager to showcase local agricultural bounty, soon dreamed up the much larger state fairs that garnered support from many counties and raised enough money to build grandstands for horse racing and exhibition halls for food and livestock. New York organized the nation's first state fair in Syracuse in 1846. By the 1860s, state and county fairs were being held all across the country, usually to celebrate the end of the harvest, to provide a place to see and be seen, and to bring city and rural folks and farmers together. And they have never gone out of style or lost their ability to delight and entertain us. Many fairs proudly claim to have been held for one hundred years or more, and state fairs have become multimillion-dollar extravaganzas sprawling for acres and acres.

Minnesta
STATE FAIR

MINNESOTA CENTENNIAL
1858 1958

CENTENNIAL EXPOSITION

1958 Princess Kay of
the Milky Way — Miss
Judy Merritt of Lakeville,
Minnesota.

SANCTIONED BY

INTERNATIONAL MOTOR CONTEST ASSN.
AMERICA'S OLDEST

INDEX

	Page
Speedway events	6
Speedway entry list	8
Stock car events	7
Stock car entry list	9
General information	12
Auto race information	14
Motorcycle entry list	24
Race records	15
Race score sheets	20-21
Kids' bicycle derby	26
Midget entry list	19
Thrill show program	34
Night show program	30-31
State Fair map	33

25¢

7

Spectators have always come to fairs to see extraordinary sights. Shock and awe were and are part of the experience. At the turn of the twentieth century, carefully calibrated locomotive collisions delighted fairgoers, as did trained dogs, pigs, and horses that plunged off platforms into tanks of water. Wing-walkers balanced on biplanes in the 1920s, daredevils drove cars into burning buildings in the 1930s, and later on, demolition derbies added to the pandemonium. Many fairs ceased operation during World War II, and when they started up again, they became tamer. Today, we watch bareback horse races, harness races, motorcycle races, lawnmower races, antique tractor parades, country and western concerts, and high-school marching band competitions. Other silly and curious spectacles mimic circus sideshows: swine agility contests, the two-thousand-pound steer, a one-thousand-pound pumpkin, and even a grilled-cheese-sandwich-eating champion and a parade of "hot rod" tractors.

Whatever we witness, we are always eating mind-boggling and traditional delights: deep-fried Twinkies, cotton candy, roasted corn, gumbo, funnel cakes, giant turkey legs, cream puffs, candy apples, barbecue, fried chicken, alligator on a stick, date

LOS ANGELES COUNTY *Fair*

AMERICA'S GREATEST

POMONA · SEPT. 12 TO 28

1941

Fair Facts and Guide

Feature PRESENTATION

Official SOUVENIR PROGRAM 25c

YORK INTER STATE *FAIR*

SEPTEMBER 14-15-16-17-18 1948

5 DAYS 5 NIGHTS

COMPLETE LIST OF EVENTS

shakes, and snow cones. And, if we're lucky, there will be a butter sculpture, an old-time folk art now being revived at fairs all across the country. In 1903, dairy companies introduced cows and other subjects made entirely of butter and displayed in refrigerated cases: great eight-hundred-pound monuments of saturated fat. Teddy Roosevelt was sculpted in butter in 1910 at the Minnesota State Fair, where since 1953, the Midwest Dairy Association has chosen to honor a Princess Kay of the Milky Way by sculpting a portrait bust of her in butter.

State and county fairs present a rare opportunity for exhibitors to proudly show off and be recognized for an astounding array of superlatives: the perfect pie, the most obedient ox, the best harmonica tune, the tallest sunflower, the most beautiful baby, the longest-crowing rooster, the tastiest chili, the hugest hog, the fastest duck, the sweetest fudge, the farthest-spit watermelon seed.

In the pages that follow, we honor one of the oldest attractions of both state and county fairs: the chance of taking home a blue ribbon for a recipe baked at home or made in front of the fair judges. Our prizewinning recipes come from every

state and include pies, cakes, breads, candy, pickles, jam, salads, and even main dishes. The winners range from bakers as young as ten, who have won their first ribbon, to octogenarians with a room full of awards. The recipes will give you tastes of many different events, from the three-day Deltana Fair in the heart of the Alaska wilderness to the twenty-four-day Texas State Fair extravaganza, just two miles from downtown Dallas. Best of all, you never have to wait until July 20 or August 15 or September 30 for the gates to open. Whenever you're in the mood, you can simply head to the kitchen and re-create a prizewinner.

DELAWARE COUNTY *Fair*

1852 ★ 1952

PRICE—10 CENTS

"For Home and Country"

NINETY-THIRD ANNUAL

THE GREAT DARKE COUNTY FAIR

The Largest County Fair on Earth

Presents this Premium List, Rules and Regulations Covering Awards

DAY AND NIGHT

AUGUST 22,23,24,25,26,27, 1948

GREENVILLE, OHIO

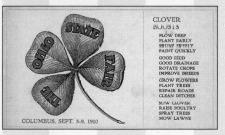

OHIO STATE FAIR

COLUMBUS, SEPT. 5-9, 1910

CLOVER BOOSTS

PLOW DEEP
PLANT EARLY
DRINE FREELY
PAINT QUICKLY

GOOD SEED
GOOD DRAINAGE
ROTATE CROPS
IMPROVE BREEDS

GROW FLOWERS
PLANT TREES
REPAIR ROADS
CLEAN DITCHES

SOW CLOVER
RAISE POULTRY
SPRAY TREES
MOW LAWNS

Mary's Sticky Biscuits

First place in the Best Biscuit Contest sponsored by Alaga Syrup at the Alabama National Fair in Montgomery went to Sandi Klinger for these tasty biscuits. Serve them as a breakfast treat along with fresh fruit and eggs. Since 1953, the fair has been important to the local community, and it is attended yearly by approximately 225,000 people. Spreading out in the Garrett Coliseum, which includes twenty-two horse barns and a twenty-acre paved parking area with tie space for fifteen hundred cattle, the ten-day event in mid-October offers plenty to see: specific shows for Hereford, Charolais, Angus, and Brahman cattle; stunts of racing and diving pigs; llama-cart driving; a live shark encounter; and contests for baking as well as cooking chicken, beef, and Cajun food.

BROWN SUGAR–ORANGE GLAZE
4   tablespoons butter
¼   cup fresh orange juice
½   cup packed light brown sugar
1   tablespoon grated orange zest

BISCUITS
2   cups all-purpose flour
1   tablespoon baking powder
½   teaspoon salt
½   cup vegetable oil
¾   cup whole milk

FILLING
¼   cup packed light brown sugar
½   teaspoon ground cinnamon
¼   teaspoon ground allspice

Heat the oven to 450°F. Grease an 8-inch square baking pan.

To make the glaze: Combine all the ingredients in a small saucepan, bring to a boil, and set aside for a few minutes until the butter melts. Pour the mixture into the prepared pan.

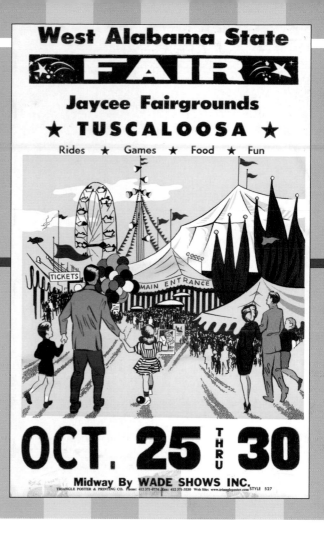

To make the biscuits: Combine the flour, baking powder, and salt in a large bowl and whisk until mixed. Make a well in the center. Combine the oil and milk in a small bowl and whisk until blended. Pour the milk mixture into the well in the dry ingredients and stir until a soft dough forms. Transfer the dough to a lightly floured work surface and roll into a 10-by-18-inch rectangle.

To make the filling: Combine all the ingredients in a small bowl and stir with a fork until blended. Sprinkle evenly over the rectangle. Starting from a long side, roll up the rectangle jelly-roll-style into an 18-inch-long cylinder. Slice into 9 biscuits, each about 2 inches thick. Arrange the biscuits, cut-side down, in 3 rows on top of the glaze in the pan.

Bake for 20 minutes, or until puffed and golden. Immediately invert the pan onto a large platter so the glaze runs down over the biscuits. Serve hot.

Makes 9 biscuits

Variation: Add ½ cup chopped walnuts or pecans to the glaze before pouring it into the pan.

Melody's Molasses Crinkles

Melody Holbrook won a ribbon for these old-fashioned favorites at the Deltana Fair in Delta Junction, a farming community in the heart of the Alaska wilderness. Be sure to allow time for the dough to chill, an important step in making it easy to work with and achieving the lovely crackled appearance. Held each year at the end of July, the fair shows off the best of the area's farm animals, and offers contests in hamburger eating, pie eating, and guessing where the cow patties will fall. There are also rides, games, flower and quilt displays, and a beautiful-baby competition. If you visit, stop at the Visitors Center to arrange a tour of a nearby farm.

½	cup (1 stick) butter, softened
2	cups packed light brown sugar
2	eggs
½	cup dark molasses
4½	cups all-purpose flour
4	teaspoons baking soda
½	teaspoon salt
1	teaspoon ground cloves
2	teaspoons ground ginger
2	teaspoons ground cinnamon

Combine the butter, sugar, eggs, and molasses in a medium bowl and beat thoroughly. Combine all the remaining ingredients in a medium bowl and stir with a whisk. Stir or gently beat the dry ingredients into the butter mixture to form a dry and crumbly batter. Refrigerate for at least 4 hours, or preferably overnight.

Heat the oven to 375°F. In your palm, roll the dough into 1-inch balls and place 3 inches apart on an ungreased baking sheet. Bake for 10 to 12 minutes, or until the cookies are set but not hard. Transfer them to a wire rack to cool.

Makes 5 to 6 dozen cookies

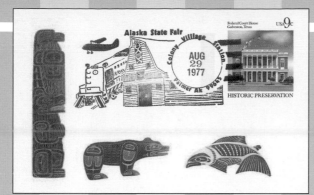

COME TO THE FUR RENDEZVOUS

ANCHORAGE, FEB. 18-21

ALASKA MAPS

ALASKA STEAMSHIP COMPANY
Serving All Alaska

Citrus Cowboy Creams

Among the various cooking contests at the Arizona State Fair in Phoenix, one of the most popular is the Arizona Candy Shoppe, sponsored by C&H Sugar, a one-hundred-year-old company that has participated in the fair for many years. Contestants are asked to create a candy that reminds them of Arizona, with its citrus trees, palm trees, Native Americans, Hispanic culture, colorful history, and Southwest flavor. First-prize winner, Maria Baldwin of Mesa, represented her state with these lightly orange-scented chocolates, which are delightful when made into Western shapes. The fair traces its history back to 1884. Offering family-centered events, it features a wide variety of animals, including miniature horses, pigeons, and prize cattle; amusement rides; and several eating contests, among them the World Grilled Cheese Eating Championship. Displays currently include the revival of an old American fair tradition: a sculpture made entirely of butter.

2½	cups sugar
1	cup milk
¼	cup light corn syrup
2	tablespoons butter
	Pinch of salt
1	teaspoon orange extract
	Few drops of orange food coloring
2	ounces white chocolate, chopped
2	ounces dark chocolate, chopped
4	ounces milk chocolate, chopped

Butter a 9-by-13-inch baking pan. Combine the sugar, milk, corn syrup, butter, and salt in a large saucepan. Stir and cook over medium heat until the mixture reaches the soft-ball stage (238°F or when a drop of syrup forms a soft ball when dropped into a cup of cold water). Pour the syrup into the prepared pan and let it sit undisturbed until cool, at least 30 minutes.

Scrape the mixture into a medium bowl, add the orange extract and food coloring, and beat until it hardens, about 10 minutes. Transfer the

orange cream mixture from the bowl to a clean work surface and knead for a few minutes until it becomes very soft. Wrap in plastic and set aside.

Melt the three different chocolates in separate double boilers or small saucepans over hot water. Using Western-themed plastic candy molds such as boots, saddles, covered wagons, etc., paint designs in the molds with small brushes dipped into the melted chocolates,

forming stripes, dots, and other designs from the different chocolates. Refrigerate the coated molds to harden for 30 minutes.

Fill the molds with the orange cream and cover with a layer of milk chocolate. Refrigerate until firm, about 1 hour, and remove from the molds. If the candies are hard to unmold, freeze the molds for about 30 minutes and then unmold.

Makes 3 to 4 dozen candies, depending on the size of the molds

Jackpot Cherry Pie

One of the most popular contests at the Arkansas State Fair in Little Rock is the First Lady's Pie Contest, with all the entries based on a theme chosen by the governor's wife. When First Lady Janet Huckabee decided on cherry pie, there was stiff competition among the meringue fillings, meringue tops, almond tops, and chocolate crusts. Terry Sue Satkowski of North Little Rock won first prize and $250 for this innovative lattice-top pie, which uses three different kinds of cherries. Held for ten days in mid-October, the fair dates back to the 1860s and can count on 400,000 patrons. Its livestock show and 4-H livestock auction are especially big draws, along with the ten-acre midway, a talent show, karaoke contests, and high-diving performances.

SOUTHWEST ARKANSAS FAIR
SEPTEMBER 22-27
★ HOPE

CRUST

2	cups all-purpose flour
1	teaspoon salt
¾	cup vegetable shortening (preferably nonhydrogenated)
4	to 5 tablespoons cold water
1	teaspoon cherry extract

CHERRY FILLING

One	14-ounce can pitted dark sweet cherries
One	14-ounce can pitted sour cherries
One	6-ounce jar maraschino cherries
	Juice of 1 lemon
1½	teaspoons cherry extract
1½	cups sugar
½	teaspoon red food coloring
¼	teaspoon vanilla extract
3	tablespoons instant tapioca
¼	cup cherry butter or cherry preserves
2	tablespoons butter for dotting
1	tablespoon milk
1	tablespoon red-tinted sugar

To make the crust: Sift the flour and salt together into a medium bowl. Add the shortening and cut it into the dry ingredients with a pastry blender, 2 dinner knives, or your fingertips. Combine 4 tablespoons of the water and the cherry extract in a small bowl and add to the flour 1 tablespoonful at a time to form a soft dough. Add the remaining 1 tablespoon of water if necessary to form a dough that can be formed into a ball. Divide the dough into 2 equal portions. Roll one portion to an 11-inch circle and fit it into a 9-inch pie pan. Roll the remaining dough into another 11-inch circle and cut it into 1-inch-wide strips for a lattice top. Set aside.

To make the filling: Pour all three kinds of cherries into a colander set over a bowl and drain. Reserve ¾ cup of the juices. Transfer the cherries to a medium bowl. Add the lemon juice, cherry extract, and ¾ cup of the sugar and stir gently with a rubber spatula. Set aside for at least 15 minutes.

Heat the oven to 425°F. Combine the reserved ¾ cup of cherry juices with the remaining ¾ cup sugar, the food coloring, and vanilla in a saucepan over medium heat. Cook for about 4 minutes, or until heated through. Add the tapioca and cook for about 5 minutes longer, stirring constantly, until the mixture thickens. Pour the tapioca mixture into the cherries and stir until blended. Spread the cherry butter or preserves evenly over the bottom of the prepared crust and pour in the cherry filling. Dot the filling with butter. Arrange the dough strips in a lattice pattern on top of the filling and flute the edges of the pie. Brush the lattice with milk and sprinkle the red sugar on top.

Place the pie in the lower rack of the oven and bake for 15 minutes. Turn the heat down to 375°F, move the pie to the upper oven rack, and bake for 35 to 40 minutes longer, or until the filling is bubbly and the crust is golden. During the last 20 to 25 minutes of cooking time, cover the rim of the crust with aluminum foil to prevent burning.

Makes one 9-inch pie; serves 6 to 8

Variation: If you prefer a tart pie, reduce the total quantity of sugar to ⅔ cup and use ⅓ cup of sugar for each of the additions.

Salsa Jam

Linda J. Amendt of Murrieta has earned over nine hundred awards, including more than six hundred blue ribbons and special awards for excellence, in food competitions at state and county fairs. She created this recipe for family members and friends who wanted a jam with zip and zing. This beautifully colored, festive spread earned top honors in the special jam competition at the California State Fair in Sacramento, where the judges declared it "an A+ jam!" Linda stresses the importance of stirring the jam as much as the recipe says, since it can easily burn. Running for twenty-five days from mid-August to early September, the state fair can trace its history to 1854. Its largest competitive programs are still agricultural, and many visitors come to see the horse shows and livestock exhibits. There are also plenty of rides and games, a "Celebrate California" contest for scrapbook designers, a woodworking competition, a giant sand sculpture, and contests for baking, cooking, and the best local wine, cheese, beer, and fine art.

1½	pounds ripe plum tomatoes, peeled, seeded, and chopped (2 cups)
⅔	cup chopped red onion
⅔	cup tomato sauce
3	tablespoons seeded and minced jalapeño chile
1½	teaspoons grated lime zest
3	tablespoons strained fresh lime juice
¼	teaspoon Tabasco sauce or other hot pepper sauce
5	cups sugar
One	3-ounce pouch liquid pectin

Combine the tomatoes, onion, tomato sauce, and chile in an 8-quart stainless-steel kettle. Bring the mixture to a boil over medium heat, stirring constantly. Reduce the heat to medium-low and simmer gently for 5 minutes, stirring frequently to prevent sticking. Add the lime zest, lime juice, and hot pepper sauce. Gradually stir in the sugar. Heat the mixture, stirring constantly, until the sugar is completely

dissolved. Increase the heat to medium-high and, stirring constantly, bring the mixture to a full rolling boil. Stir in the contents of the pectin pouch. Return the mixture to a full rolling boil, stirring constantly. Cook, stirring constantly, for 1 minute. Remove the pan from the heat.

To prevent the jam from separating in the jars, allow it to cool for 5 minutes before filling the jars. As it is cooling, gently stir the jam every minute or so to distribute the salsa. Ladle the hot jam into hot, sterilized jars, leaving ¼-inch headspace. Wipe the jar rims and threads with a clean, damp cloth. Cover with hot, sterilized lids and rings. Seal tightly. Process in a boiling-water bath for 10 minutes. Let cool for 24 hours. Wash jars, dry thoroughly, and store in a cool, dark place for up to 12 months.

Makes about 5 half-pints

Note: Linda, who has become a judge for fairs, has written the book on making jam: *Blue Ribbon Preserves: Secrets to Award-Winning Jams, Jellies, Marmalades & More.* Copies are available online at www.blueribbonpreserves.com.

Colorado Potato Cream Pie

Laura Milosavich of Pueblo won first place in the Colorado Potato Contest at the 2004 Colorado State Fair for this savory pie, which goes nicely with roast chicken or steak and is surprisingly good cold. The fair, which runs for ten days from late August to early September, traces its history to the Southern Colorado Agricultural and Industrial Association Show held at Lake Minnequa in 1872. At the turn of the century, the exposition moved to its present eighty-acre site in Pueblo. The architecture of the fair buildings is impressive: from 1920 to 1930, red-brick exhibition, poultry, and cattle buildings were constructed; and in 1934, native stone quarried just a few miles from the fairgrounds was used to build the landmark hog and sheep barn, 365 feet long and 100 feet wide, as well as racing facilities with 215 separate stable rooms. Current-day fair events include a concert series; five nights of professional rodeo shows; fifteen hundred categories of arts, crafts, and food competitions; extensive carnival rides; and plenty of prize farm animals to admire.

3	tablespoons butter
1	small onion, diced
3	large Colorado russet potatoes, cooked, peeled, and shredded
3	green onion tops, chopped
1½	cups sour cream
One	10½-ounce can cream of chicken soup
1	cup (4 ounces) shredded sharp Cheddar cheese
½	teaspoon salt
¼	teaspoon ground white pepper
	Unbaked pastry for a 2-crust pie
	Garlic salt to taste (optional)

Heat the oven to 425°F. Melt the butter in a small saucepan over low heat. Add the onion and sauté for 3 minutes, or until tender. Remove from the heat. Place the potatoes in a large bowl and add the sautéed onion and the green onion tops. Combine the sour cream and soup in a

small bowl and add to the potato mixture along with the cheese, salt, and pepper. Stir until smooth.

Roll out the bottom pie crust and line a 9-inch pie pan. Spoon the mixture into the pie shell. Roll out the top crust, place it over the filling, and flute the edges. Cut slits or a design in the top. Bake for 20 to 25 minutes, or until golden brown. Sprinkle garlic salt on the top crust before serving, if desired. Serve warm.

Makes one 9-inch pie; serves 6 to 8

Variation: To reduce the fat, sauté the onion in 2 teaspoons of olive oil and use reduced-fat sour cream. To reduce the sodium, substitute 1 can of cream of mushroom soup that contains less than 400 grams of sodium per serving for the cream of chicken soup.

Note: Fair officials have published a cookbook containing 500 winning recipes from past years. To order a copy of the *Colorado State Fair Who's Cookin' Cookbook* ($15 plus $5 shipping and handling), call the General Entry Office, 719-404-2080.

Country Fair "Caramel Apples"

In the tradition of the very early regional agricultural events, the Association of Connecticut Fairs makes several recipes available to contestants in their various cooking contest divisions. All entrants follow the specific recipe, and judges choose the best in each category. A recent Junior Baking Contest, open to anyone between the ages of nine and fifteen, offered $15 and a rosette to the best batch of these cupcakes, which masquerade as candy apples. The Association of Connecticut Fairs counts fifty-three member fairs that are held each year in the eight counties. They include major events that draw thousands of people, as well as 4-H and grange fairs attended by a few hundred. The main cooking competitions are open to Connecticut residents who attend any fair belonging to the Association.

1⅔	cups all-purpose flour
1	cup packed light brown sugar
1	teaspoon ground cinnamon
½	teaspoon ground allspice
1	teaspoon baking soda
½	teaspoon salt
¾	cup applesauce
¼	cup sour cream
⅓	cup vegetable oil
1	tablespoon fresh lemon juice

CARAMEL GLAZE

20	caramels
3	tablespoons milk
½	cup finely chopped toasted walnuts

Heat the oven to 350°F. Combine the flour, sugar, cinnamon, allspice, baking soda, and salt in a medium bowl and stir with a whisk. Stir in the applesauce, sour cream, oil, and lemon juice. Spoon the batter into 12 muffin cups fitted with paper liners. Bake for 20 minutes, or until the

tops are firm to the touch. Remove from the oven and let cool on a wire rack in the pan.

To make the caramel glaze: Combine the caramels and milk in a small saucepan and cook over low heat, stirring frequently, for about 5 minutes, or until the caramels are melted and the mixture is smooth. Pour about 1 tablespoon of warm glaze over the top of each cupcake, smoothing it with a knife if necessary to cover the top evenly. Garnish each cupcake with walnuts to resemble a caramel apple dipped in nuts. Insert a Popsicle stick in the center of each muffin and serve.

Makes 12 muffins

N728:-A FINE RED APPLE

Lakeshore Italian Steak and Potato Salad

Second prize in the 2005 Beef and Potato Cook-Off Contest at the Delaware State Fair went to Bonnie Robinson for this main-course salad, which is tossed with warm dressing and makes a lovely lunch dish. She won a $200 gift certificate to spend on beef at a local market. The fair, held in Harrington, began in 1920 as the Kent and Sussex County Fair, which made a net profit of $43.90 its first year. Since then it has grown into a ten-day exposition that draws more than 270,000 visitors, who come to see extensive livestock displays, harness racing, the crowning of the Lamb and Wool Queen, a table-setting competition, and contests in cooking, horseshoe pitching, and rooster crowing.

2	pounds top round steak, thinly sliced
1	cup bottled raspberry vinaigrette dressing, or to taste
3	tablespoons salt
2	pounds small red-skin potatoes, cut into quarters
2	small Vidalia onions, finely sliced
½	cup water
8	slices bacon, cooked and crumbled
	Leaves from 2 heads romaine lettuce, torn into bite-sized pieces
2	cups grape tomatoes, halved
3	cups broccoli florets, cut into small pieces, raw or lightly steamed
3	tablespoons grated Parmesan cheese

Put the steak slices in a shallow baking dish, add ½ cup of the dressing, and toss to coat both sides of the meat. Cover with plastic wrap and marinate in the refrigerator for at least 1 hour and up to 24 hours. Bring a large pot of water to a boil, add the salt and the potatoes, and cook until the potatoes are soft, about 10 minutes. Drain, return to the pot, cover, and

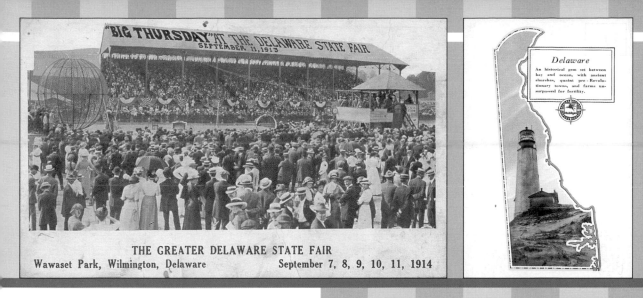

THE GREATER DELAWARE STATE FAIR
Wawaset Park, Wilmington, Delaware   September 7, 8, 9, 10, 11, 1914

set aside. Drain the meat slices and put them in a large skillet, along with the onions and water. Bring almost to a rapid simmer over high heat, reduce the heat to medium, cover, and simmer for about 5 minutes, or until the meat is no longer pink and the onions are tender. Drain and return the meat and onions to the skillet. Cover and keep warm.

Heat the remaining ½ cup of dressing in a small saucepan. Add the bacon to the potatoes and toss gently. Put the lettuce, tomatoes, and broccoli in a large salad bowl, add the potato mixture along with the steak and onions, and pour on the warm dressing. Sprinkle with the cheese and toss gently to mix.

Serves 6 to 8

Pecan Fudge Caramel Squares

For these sinfully delicious candies, Diana Doughty of Merritt Island won First Place and Best in Section awards at the Space Coast Fair in Cocoa. Beware: they are truly addictive! Cut into small pieces and share them with coworkers or neighbors. Covering seventy acres and offering more than two hundred rides, games, and shows, the ten-day fair presents a wide range of 4-H and farm exhibitions, cooking and crafts competitions, a rooster-crowing contest, bull riding, a monster truck show and race, demolition daredevils, and beer garden bands.

3	cups (12 ounces) pecan pieces, finely chopped
1/4	cup granulated sugar
4	tablespoons butter, softened
One	14-ounce bag caramels
2/3	cup heavy (whipping) cream
8	ounces semi-sweet baking chocolate, chopped
1/4	cup sifted confectioner's sugar
1/2	teaspoon vanilla extract

Heat the oven to 350°F. Combine 2 cups of the pecans with the granulated sugar and butter in a medium bowl. Mix with your fingertips until the mixture is crumbly. Press the mixture into the bottom and 1 inch up the sides of a 7-by-10 ½-inch baking pan. Bake for 15 minutes to toast the pecans and set the crust. Transfer the pan to a wire rack and let cool completely.

Combine the caramels and ⅓ cup of the cream in a small bowl and microwave for 1½ minutes. Stir and microwave for another 1½ minutes, and stir again until smooth. Pour the caramel mixture over the crust in the pan and tilt the pan slightly if necessary to form a smooth layer. Scatter on the remaining 1 cup pecans.

Combine the chocolate, the remaining ⅓ cup cream, the confectioners' sugar, and vanilla in a medium saucepan and cook over low heat, stirring frequently, for about 4 minutes, or until the chocolate has melted and the mixture is smooth. Pour evenly over the nut layer in the pan. Refrigerate for at least 2 hours to set. Cut into 1-inch squares. Store, covered, in the refrigerator.

Makes about 42 pieces

Marie Antoinettes

Rebecca Brooks of Byron won first place in the "I Love Eggs" Sweets and Treats Breakfast Contest sponsored by the Georgia Egg Commission at the Georgia National Fair in Perry. Her delicate pastries with puffy tops mimic the French heroine's hairstyle and are great fun to make. Established in 1990, the event is a relative newcomer in the American fair scene, but draws 400,000 visitors for the ten days it runs in early October. Its extensive schedule includes self-guided educational tours of a historic schoolhouse, competitions and livestock exhibitions, concerts, a magic show, a laser show, racing pigs, a rose show, a vegetable-casserole contest, and the World Hamburger Eating Championship.

One	17-ounce package frozen puff pastry, thawed
4	ounces cream cheese, softened
¼	cup lime or lemon curd
¼	cup plus 1 tablespoon granulated sugar
2	eggs
1	tablespoon water
1	cup sliced fresh strawberries
	Confectioners' sugar for dusting

Heat the oven to 400°F. Grease a mini muffin pan with 18 cups. Cut one of the pastry sheets into 18 squares (it's okay if they're not all perfectly square) and gently press one into each muffin cup. Use a small juice glass to cut tops for the pastries out of the remaining pastry sheet. Arrange the pastry rounds on a small baking sheet.

Combine the cream cheese, curd, the ¼ cup sugar, and 1 of the eggs in a small bowl and beat with a whisk until smooth. Spoon the mixture

into the pastry-lined muffin cups. Combine the remaining egg and the water in a small bowl and beat with a fork. Brush the pastry that protrudes above the filling and the tops on the baking sheet with the egg mixture. Bake the filled pastries and the tops for 10 to 12 minutes, or until the crusts are lightly browned.

In a small bowl, combine the strawberries and the 1 tablespoon of sugar. Spoon 1 or 2 strawberry slices into the pastries, place a cap on each, very gently press it down to secure, and dust with confectioners' sugar.

Makes 18 pastries

Note: Lemon curd is often sold with the jams and jellies in large supermarkets. Look for lime curd in gourmet grocery stores.

Blue Hawaiian

1	ounce dark rum
¼	ounce blue curaçao liqueur
1	ounce pineapple juice
½	ounce heavy (whipping) cream
1	teaspoon coconut cream
½	cup crushed ice

Hawaii became a state in 1959, and fairs don't figure into its unique traditions and culture. But gatherings to have fun certainly do. If you visit Hawaii in August or September, you'll most likely encounter the statewide series of three hundred events known as the Aloha Festivals. This celebration began in April 1946 as Aloha Week, and has grown into a two-month-long fall party. To honor the *makahiki,* the ancient Hawaiian time of music, dance, and feasting, there are daily hula performances, concerts, art fairs, parades, a *poke* contest (celebrating Hawaii's favorite soul food, spicy raw fish mixed with sea vegetables), exhibits, and crafts demonstrations. This cocktail was created in honor of the festive occasion.

In a cocktail shaker, combine all the ingredients and shake well. Strain into a chilled collins glass.

Serves 1

THE VALLEY ISLE

MAUI

Fireworks Display, "Volcano in Eruption."

Sourdough Bread

Charles and Connie McGuffey of Caldwell won a blue ribbon for this home-style bread at the Eastern Idaho State Fair in Blackfoot. Their secret is mixing the starter with water left over from cooking potatoes, rice, or pasta. The eight-day fair began in 1902 and has been held annually since 1944. It features more than two thousand animals, including ostriches, llamas, and emus, along with more conventional livestock, plus many baking and canning contests, and flower, antiques, and needlecraft exhibitions. One of the most popular events is the bareback Indian relay horse race. Signature snacks include giant turkey legs and funnel cakes.

2	cups sourdough starter (see Note)
2	cups lukewarm (90°F) water
7	to 9 cups all-purpose flour
1	package active dry yeast
2	cups warm (110° to 115°F) water
⅓	cup sugar
1	tablespoon salt
3	tablespoons vegetable oil or melted butter

The night before baking, combine the starter, lukewarm water, and 2 cups of the flour in a large bowl and mix well. Cover and let sit in a warm place overnight. In the morning, add the yeast to the 2 cups warm water, stir, and let stand for 10 minutes, or until foamy. Add 2 cups of the flour mixture, the sugar, salt, and oil or butter. (Pour the remaining flour mixture into a starter crock and refrigerate.) Add enough of the remaining flour to make a medium-soft but not sticky dough.

On a lightly floured work surface, knead the dough for 6 to 8 minutes, or until smooth and elastic. Place the dough in a lightly greased

bowl, turning once to coat the dough. Cover with plastic wrap and let rise in a warm place until doubled, about 1 hour. Punch down the dough, cover again, and let rise again until doubled, about 1 hour. Punch down, knead lightly, and cut into 2 pieces. Cut each piece into 3 strips and roll each out to about 12 inches long and about 1 inch thick. Braid the 3 strips, seal the ends, and place on a lightly greased baking sheet. Repeat with the remaining piece of dough and place on the same baking sheet.

Cover with a cloth and let rise again until doubled, about 1 hour.

Heat the oven to 350°F. Bake for 35 to 45 minutes, or until the crusts are lightly browned and the loaves sound hollow when gently tapped. Let cool completely on wire racks.

Makes 2 loaves; serves 8 to 10 per loaf

Note: Look for packaged sourdough starter in the baking section of your supermarket.

Soy Velvet Crumb Cake

Carolyn Rentfro of Decatur won top honors and $100 in the "Cooking for Health, Cooking with Soy" competition sponsored by the Illinois Soybean Checkoff Board at the Illinois State Fair in Springfield. Her moist cake has a decadently delicious crunchy topping and can be served as either coffee cake or a dessert. The ten-day fair, which is held in mid-August, dates back to 1853, when admission was twenty-five cents. Early fairs were held in twelve different Illinois cities before finding a permanent home in Springfield more than one hundred years ago. Offering one of the country's most extensive selections of agricultural exhibitions, the fair covers 336 acres. Visitors can wander through five theme areas, including Main Street USA and the Wild West; enjoy a free Illinois Symphony concert; watch harness racing, cooking demonstrations, and the Decorated Diaper Contest; see the four-hundred-pound butter cow; enjoy bratwurst, potato salad, and pork sandwiches; and watch the "Marriage on the Midway," when an engaged couple is selected by popular vote to be married at the fair.

CAKE

3¾	cups whole-grain soy flour
1½	cups sugar
1	teaspoon baking powder
1	teaspoon baking soda
1	teaspoon ground cinnamon
3	eggs
1½	cups plain soy milk
6	tablespoons shortening (preferably nonhydrogenated)
1	teaspoon vanilla extract

COCONUT TOPPING

1	cup sweetened flaked coconut
⅔	cup packed light brown sugar
½	teaspoon ground cinnamon
½	cup chopped pecans
6	tablespoons cold butter, cut into bits
3	tablespoons plain soy milk

Heat the oven to 350°F. Grease and flour a 10-inch springform pan.

To make the cake: Combine the flour, sugar, baking powder, baking soda, and cinnamon in a medium bowl and stir with a whisk. Add the eggs, soy milk, shortening, and vanilla and beat with an electric mixer on low speed for about 1 minute, scraping the sides of the bowl several times, until all the dry ingredients are moistened. Increase the speed to medium and beat 4 minutes more, scraping the bowl occasionally.

Pour the batter into the prepared pan, smooth the top, and bake for 40 to 45 minutes, or until a toothpick inserted in the center of the cake comes out clean. Transfer the pan to a wire rack and let cool for 3 minutes.

To make the topping: Heat the broiler. Combine all the ingredients in a medium bowl and stir with a fork to mix. Spoon the topping evenly over the warm cake. Broil 3 or 4 inches from the heat source for about 3 minutes, or until the top of the cake is deep brown. Watch closely so it doesn't burn. Let cool in the pan on a wire rack for 15 minutes. Run a knife around the edge of the cake, remove the sides of the pan, and transfer the cake to a serving plate.

Makes one 10-inch cake; serves 10 to 12

Double-Chocolate Peanut Butter Chip Cookies

Mary Schuman and her sister, Nancy, grew up on a farm in Whitley County and have been exhibiting their cookies and cakes at the Indiana State Fair in Indianapolis for close to thirty years. Here's one of Mary's prizewinning recipes, which makes delicious little cookies that are very easy to eat. The fair, which dates back to 1852, runs for eleven days, and is famous for its food, which includes roasted sweet corn; grilled cheese sandwiches; cream puffs; deep-fried Twinkies and Snickers bars; chicken, turkey, and duck barbecue; and steak sandwiches. It's also chock-full of livestock and farm exhibitions and demonstrations to celebrate the state's agricultural importance, including the judging of twenty-five thousand rabbits and a contest to determine the world's largest male hog.

$2\frac{1}{4}$	cups all-purpose flour
1	teaspoon baking soda
1	cup (2 sticks) butter, softened
$\frac{1}{4}$	cup granulated sugar
$\frac{3}{4}$	cup packed light brown sugar
1	teaspoon vanilla extract
One	$3\frac{5}{8}$-ounce package instant chocolate pudding mix
2	eggs
1	cup chocolate chips
1	cup peanut butter chips
1	cup raisins

Heat the oven to 375°F. Combine the flour and baking soda in a medium bowl and stir with a whisk. Combine the butter, sugars, vanilla, and pudding mix in a large bowl and beat until smooth and creamy. Beat in the eggs. Gradually stir in the flour mixture. Stir in the chips and raisins. (The batter will be very stiff.) Drop by

rounded teaspoonfuls about 2 inches apart on an ungreased baking sheet.

Bake for 8 to 10 minutes, or until the cookies are slightly crisp around the edges. Let the cookies sit on the baking sheet for about 5 minutes before transferring them to a wire rack to cool completely.

Makes about 6 dozen cookies

Cool Fruit Strata

The Iowa Heart Center sponsors two healthy cooking contests at the Iowa State Fair, one for kids' snacks and one for healthful family meals. Anne Nieland of Urbandale won the latter contest with this low-fat recipe. One of the country's oldest events, the fair began in 1854 and found its permanent home in Des Moines in 1879. It inspired Rodgers and Hammerstein to write the musical *State Fair,* which tells the story of Abel Frake, who set off in 1946 hoping to win a blue ribbon with his prize boar, Blue Boy. Today, the event offers the largest foods department of any U.S. fair, and draws more than 1 million visitors, who flock to enjoy corn dogs, watch stock car racing, and see the acres of livestock and agricultural exhibitions.

1	cup pineapple juice
1	tablespoon peach schnapps (optional)
1	tablespoon frozen orange juice concentrate
1	cup black or purple seedless grapes, halved
½	cantaloupe, peeled and thinly sliced
1	cup seedless green grapes, halved
2	peaches, peeled, pitted, and sliced
1	cup Bing cherries, pitted and halved
2	cups blueberries
1½	mangoes, peeled, pitted, and sliced

Bring the pineapple juice to a boil over medium-high heat in a small saucepan. Reduce the heat to medium-low and simmer for about 8 minutes, or until reduced to ¼ cup. Remove from the heat and let cool for 5 minutes. Add the

GREETINGS FROM

IOWA STATE FAIR

DES MOINES, IOWA

schnapps (if using) and the orange juice concentrate and stir until smooth. Set aside.

Layer the fruit in an 8-cup bowl (preferably glass) in the following order, sprinkling a little sauce on each layer: black grapes, cantaloupe, green grapes, peaches, cherries, blueberries, mango slices. Pour any remaining sauce over the top. Refrigerate for 2 to 8 hours.

Serves 4 to 6

Note: The 276-page *Iowa State Fair Cookbook* is packed with winning recipes from the many different fair categories. Call 515-262-3111 for details.

Strawberry Daisy Bread

Twelve-year-old Ashley Lesser baked this bread and won the Grand Champion Nonperishable Food award at the Douglas County Fair in Lawrence, Kansas. Serve it for breakfast or brunch when you have enough people around the table to make an event of pulling the petals off the daisy—and then devouring them. Douglas County established a fair association in 1868, but the present-day event was started in 1905. It attracts approximately 20,000 people to its 6,000 exhibitions, and features an outdoor movie, a bale-throwing contest, a draft-horse pull, a demolition derby, and a hot-rod tractor and truck pull.

Put the water in a mixing bowl, add the yeast, and stir until dissolved. Let stand for 10 minutes, or until foamy. Add the oil, sugar, egg, mashed potatoes, and salt and beat until well mixed. Beat in 1½ cups of the flour. Add 2 more cups of the flour and beat to form a smooth, slightly sticky dough. Transfer the dough to a floured board and knead for 5 minutes, or until smooth and elastic, working in all or part of the remaining

¾	cup warm (110° to 115°F) water
1	package active dry yeast
⅓	cup vegetable oil
⅓	cup granulated sugar
1	egg
½	cup mashed potatoes
1½	teaspoons salt
3½	to 4 cups all-purpose flour
½	to ¾ cup strawberry jam

TOPPING

⅓	cup all-purpose flour
¼	cup granulated sugar
2	tablespoons butter, softened

FROSTING

1	tablespoon butter
1	cup sifted confectioners' sugar
½	teaspoon vanilla extract
3	to 4 teaspoons milk or cream

½ cup flour as needed. Lightly grease a large bowl, add the dough, and turn until the dough is

lightly coated. Cover the bowl with plastic wrap and let rise in a warm place for 1½ hours. Punch the dough down, cover again, and let rise until doubled, about 30 minutes. Punch down again and divide in half.

Grease two 12-inch pizza pans. Roll one half of the dough into a cylinder about 20 inches long and cut into 10 roughly equal pieces. Put 2 pieces together and shape into a ball to form the center of the daisy. Place it in the center of the pizza pan. Shape the remaining 8 pieces of dough into oblongs and position in the pan radiating out from the center to resemble flower petals. Flatten slightly, leaving room for the bread to rise. Repeat with the remaining dough to make a second daisy bread. Cover each pan with a cloth and let rise until doubled, about 30 minutes.

Heat the oven to 350°F. Using your thumb or a finger, make an indentation in each petal and in the center of each daisy. Fill each indentation with several teaspoons of jam.

To make the topping: Combine all the ingredients in a small bowl and mix with a fork or your fingertips until crumbly. Sprinkle half of the topping over each daisy. Bake the breads for 20 minutes, or until lightly browned. Let cool slightly on wire racks.

To make the frosting: Melt the butter over low heat in a small saucepan. Remove from the heat, add the confectioners' sugar and vanilla, and stir in 1 teaspoon of the milk. Add the remaining milk by teaspoons until the mixture is creamy. Drizzle half the frosting over each bread.

Makes 2 loaves; serves 18 to 20

Aunt Betsy's Bourbon Chowder with Onion-Pita Rounds

Trudy Hunt won first place in the Evan Williams Bourbon Cooking Contest at the Kentucky State Fair for this fragrant and delicious chowder, accompanied with stuffed pita bread. Fayette County farmer Colonel Lewis Sanders organized Kentucky's first fair and stock show in 1816, but it wasn't until 1902 that the first official state fair was organized at Churchill Downs, which became the fair's permanent home in 1908. In addition to fine horse and livestock shows, displays include baked goods, homemade wines, antiques, fruits, and nuts. There are special events for seniors, a livestock auction, and the adjacent Six Flags amusement park.

Sauté the salt pork in a Dutch oven over medium heat, stirring frequently, for about 3 minutes, or until it sizzles. Add the onion(s) and half of the bourbon and continue cooking until the

12	ounces salt pork, diced
1	to 2 onions, chopped
1/3	cup bourbon
One	12-ounce can cocktail clams with juice
One	7-ounce can lump crabmeat with juice
4	potatoes, cooked and cut into bite-sized pieces
8	large shrimp, peeled and halved crosswise
1/2	pound sea scallops, halved crosswise
1/2	pound meaty white fish, preferably halibut, cut into bite-sized pieces
3	cups half-and-half
1/2	to 1 teaspoon ground black pepper

ONION-PITA ROUNDS

2	onion-pita breads
1	cup (4 ounces) shredded Monterey Jack cheese
3	tablespoons butter, softened
1	teaspoon bourbon

A photograph of the Sugar Creek Creamery Company's exhibit at the Kentucky State Fair, September, 1932. A life-size reproduction modeled by J. E. Wallace, Sculptor.

onion(s) are soft and the salt pork is browned, about 5 minutes. Drain off the fat. Drain the clams and the crabmeat, reserving the juice. Add the clam juice, crab juice, and remaining bourbon to the onion mixture and simmer for 8 to 10 minutes. Add the potatoes, clams, crabmeat, shrimp, scallops, fish, half-and-half, and pepper. Cook for about 6 minutes over medium heat, stirring very gently a few times, to heat all the ingredients. Do not let the chowder boil or it will curdle.

Meanwhile, make the pita rounds. Heat the oven to 350°F. Cut the pita breads into quarters, making 8 pieces. Fill each pocket with cheese and arrange them on a baking sheet. Combine the butter and bourbon in a small bowl and blend with a spoon. Brush the mixture on the pitas and bake for about 5 minutes, or until golden brown. Serve alongside the chowder.

Serves 4

Pickled Okra

Alice Cormier of Alexandria won a blue ribbon at the State Fair of Louisiana for these colorful pickles, which her mother always made for fair-day picnic lunches. Serve them well chilled, with sandwiches or cold meats. Founded in 1906, the fourteen-day fair in Shreveport now covers 157 acres with its extensive livestock exhibitions, and judged quilt, crochet, knitting, crafts, woodworking, and cooking events. Visitors can watch a diving show, a talent contest, a BB-gun competition, or a giant alligator and crocodile presentation, and fill up on traditional Louisiana favorites: shrimp on a stick, gator on a stick, seafood gumbo, and ribbon fries.

$3\frac{1}{2}$	to 4 pounds okra, pods no longer than 4 inches
$2\frac{1}{2}$	cups distilled white vinegar
$2\frac{1}{2}$	cups cider vinegar
1	cup water
$\frac{1}{3}$	cup canning salt
6	small sprigs dill
6	cloves garlic, sliced lengthwise into quarters
6	small serrano chiles, halved and seeded
6	small jalapeño chiles, halved and seeded

Arrange 6 hot, sterilized pint Mason jars on the counter, with 6 hot, sterilized lids and rings nearby. Rinse the okra in lukewarm water and remove any long, tough stems, keeping the pods whole. Combine the vinegars, water, and salt in a large saucepan and bring to a boil over medium-high heat. While the vinegar is heating, put 1 dill sprig in the bottom of each jar. Distribute the okra, garlic, and chiles among the jars, keeping the chiles toward the outside so their colors will show. Ladle the boiling vinegar mixture into the jars, leaving about ¼ inch of space at the top. Wipe the tops and threads of the jars with a clean, damp cloth, put on the lids and loosely screw on the rings. Let the jars cool slightly. Tighten the rings and process in a boiling-water bath for 10 minutes. Remove the jars from the hot water and let them sit on the counter until they cool and the lids have sealed.

Makes 6 pints

New York–Style Half-Sour Pickles

Adam Tomash has perfected the art of making deli-style pickles, and his recipe was an award winner at the Common Ground County Fair in Unity. Held the third weekend after Labor Day each year, the event began in 1977 and attracts some 60,000 visitors to its beautifully landscaped grounds, which are also home to the Maine Organic Farmers and Gardeners Association. Celebrating the art of living lightly on the land, the fair includes livestock exhibits, energy and shelter products, folk arts, Maine-grown organic foods, spinning, weaving, stone cutting and carving displays, and inspiring talks and information-sharing sessions so that every visitor goes home with at least one new idea.

About 5 pounds pickling cucumbers, or enough to fill a 1-gallon jar (see Note)

4 to 12 heads fresh dill

1 large onion, coarsely chopped

¼ cup pickling salt

2 to 6 cloves garlic

4 teaspoons brown mustard seed, or 2 teaspoons brown and 2 teaspoons black mustard seed

4 teaspoons pickling spice

1 small dried red pepper (optional)

Wash the cucumbers in cold water, brushing or scrubbing to remove dirt and spines. Drain well. Put a quarter of the dill and a quarter of the onion in the bottom of a 1-gallon glass or food-grade plastic jar with a nonmetallic lid. Layer one-third of the cucumbers on top. Repeat twice. Place the remaining dill and onion on top of the cucumbers. Fill the jar with filtered water to the very top.

Put the salt in a stainless-steel pot large enough to hold all the water from the jar. Put the garlic through a garlic press, letting the pressings fall on the salt. Mash the garlic into the salt and mix well. Pour the water from the pickle jar into the pot, stir, and bring almost to a boil. (It will foam over if left unattended.) Remove from the heat and let cool to about 170°F.

Grand Stand, Maine State Fair Grounds, Lewiston, Maine.

Place the mustard seed, pickling spice, and red pepper (if using) on top of the cucumbers. Shake the jar to get some of the seeds down toward the bottom. Ladle the hot pickle water mixture very slowly over the cucumbers. It should fill the jar right to the brim. Screw on the lid. Let the jar sit at room temperature overnight. The next morning, refrigerate it for at least 2 days or up to 3 weeks.

Makes about 20 pickles

Note: Use cucumbers that are about 4 inches long. Depending on their size, you can get 16 to 24 into the jar.

Squash Pie

At the age of seventy-eight, Johanna Saghy won eight ribbons for her baked goods at the Anne Arundel County Fair in Crownsville. She had been released from the hospital the week before, and decided to help herself recover from surgery by doing some serious competition baking. After the fair, she received dozens of requests for this recipe. Both agriculture and home arts have been celebrated at the mid-September fair since 1952. The all-volunteer staff puts together a full schedule of events and activities, including duck races, car races, line dancing, a pet parade, and demonstrations on candle making and honey extracting.

1	unbaked 9-inch pie crust
2	small summer squash, peeled and shredded (2 cups)
1½	cups sugar
1	teaspoon cornstarch
1	teaspoon vanilla extract
1	teaspoon coconut extract
1	tablespoon all-purpose flour
3	eggs, slightly beaten
4	tablespoons butter, melted
	Pinch of salt

Heat the oven to 400°F. Line a 9-inch pie pan with the pastry. Combine all the remaining ingredients in a large bowl. Mix well with a spoon and pour into the unbaked crust. Bake for 10 minutes. Reduce the oven temperature to 350°F and bake for 25 minutes. Cover the edges of the crust with a pie crust shield or strips of aluminum foil to keep it from getting too brown and bake 25 to 35 minutes longer, or until the pie is evenly browned and the filling doesn't jiggle when you gently move the pan from side to side. Transfer the pie to a wire rack and let cool for 1 hour before serving.

Makes one 9-inch pie; serves 6 to 8

Variation: This recipe makes a very sweet pie. Reduce the sugar to ¾ cup if you don't have a sweet tooth.

SOUVENIR PROGRAM 25¢

STATE FAIR

"...it's a family affair!"

VISIT ANNAPOLIS
THE GATEWAY TO THE SOUTH

MARYLAND STATE HOUSE
BUILT IN 1772

61

Mini Raspberry Truffle Cakes

Here's a first-place-winning recipe from the chocolate dessert contest at the Marshfield Fair. It was created by Susan Lyonsfrom, who served each cake topped with shaved white chocolate, a lovely but optional flourish. One of the largest fairs in New England, the event was started in 1867. It is beloved for its extensive arts and crafts collections, horticultural displays, and 4-H competitions. Along with horse-pulling contests, there are also nightly concerts and a demolition derby.

16	ounces semisweet chocolate, cut into small pieces
½	cup (1 stick) butter
1	tablespoon sugar
1½	teaspoons all-purpose flour
4	eggs, separated
1	cup seedless raspberry jam
½	cup heavy cream, whipped
1	pint fresh raspberries
½	cup shaved white chocolate (optional)

Heat the oven to 350°F. Grease 6 mini cake pans (3 inches in diameter, 2 inches deep) or a 6-muffin pan with 3-inch cups, or 6 custard cups. Combine the chocolate and butter in a large, heavy saucepan and cook over low heat, stirring frequently, until they melt, about 4 minutes. Remove the pan from the heat and stir in the sugar and flour. Beat in the egg yolks, one at a time, with a spoon until well mixed. Set the mixture aside.

In a large bowl, beat the egg whites with an electric mixer on high speed or with a hand beater until stiff, glossy peaks form. Gently fold the whites into the chocolate mixture. Pour the batter into the pans or muffin or custard cups and bake for 15 minutes, or until the tops are firm and look dry. Let cool on a wire rack for 10 minutes. Run a sharp knife around the edges of the cakes and unmold them onto a platter. Cover with plastic wrap and refrigerate for at least 2 hours.

To serve, melt the jam in a small saucepan over medium-low heat and drizzle some of it on each dessert plate. Put a cake on each plate. Top with the whipped cream, raspberries, and white chocolate, if desired.

Serves 6

Pasties

Donna Jean Pomeroy of Rapid River created these prizewinning hearty meat pies at the Upper Peninsula State Fair in Escanaba. They were traditionally made for the local miners' lunch pails. Started in 1928, the fair celebrates the agricultural heritage of the Upper Peninsula and enjoys broad-based community support. It treats visitors to the atmosphere of an old-time country fair, with displays of skills such as cow calling, and exhibitions that honor the important local farming, fishing, and mining industries. It includes a timber show, a one-acre "pocket park" with a lake in the shape of the Upper Peninsula, a real fire tower for kids to climb, and plenty of great homemade food.

FILLING
- ¼ pound ground pork
- ½ pound ground beef
- 2 potatoes, peeled and chopped
- 2 carrots, peeled and chopped
- 1 cup chopped cabbage
- 2 onions, chopped
- ½ teaspoon salt
- ½ teaspoon garlic powder
- ¼ teaspoon ground black pepper
- 1 can cream of mushroom soup (preferably low sodium)

PASTRY
- 5 cups all-purpose flour
- ¾ cup shortening (preferably nonhydrogenated)
- 1 cup (2 sticks) butter
- 1 cup cold water

To make the filling: Brown the pork and beef over medium heat in a large skillet, stirring occasionally, for 5 minutes, or until most of the pink color disappears. Drain off the fat and put the meat in a medium bowl. Add the remaining ingredients and toss with a spatula until well blended. (The mixture can be cooled, covered, and stored in the refrigerator for several hours until ready to use.)

To make the pastry: Combine the flour, shortening, and butter in a large bowl and mix with a pastry blender, 2 dinner knives, or your fingertips until

continued

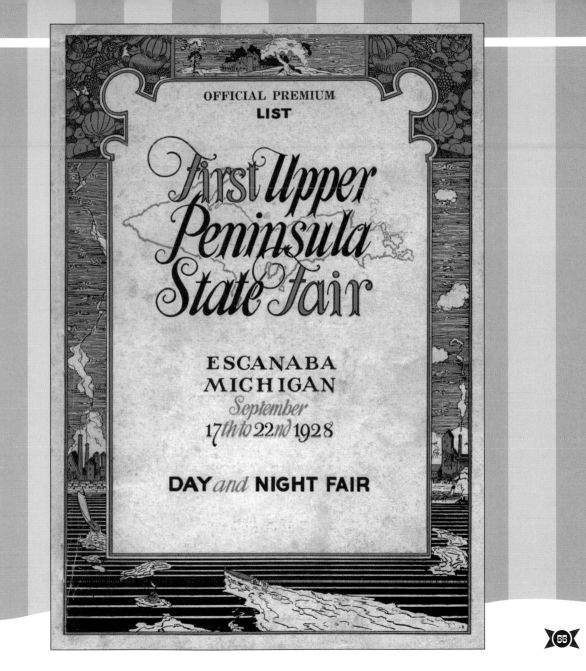

OFFICIAL PREMIUM
LIST

First Upper Peninsula State Fair

ESCANABA
MICHIGAN
September
17th to 22nd 1928

DAY *and* **NIGHT FAIR**

the mixture is crumbly and no pieces are larger than a pea. Add the cold water and stir until the mixture forms a dough. Let stand for 10 minutes.

Heat the oven to 350°F. Lightly grease a baking sheet. Measure the dough into ½-cup pieces a little smaller than a tennis ball. Roll one piece out into an 8-inch circle. Add ⅔ cup of filling to the center of the circle, keeping the filling away from the edges. Bring the dough up and over

the filling so it is completely enclosed, forming a semicircle. Crimp the edges with a fork and carefully transfer the pastie to the baking sheet. Repeat to make a total of 8 pasties.

Bake for 1 hour. Let cool for 10 minutes on the baking sheet, then transfer them to wire racks to cool.

Makes 8 pasties

Marjorie Johnson's Sour Cream Streusel Coffee Cake

In the world of state fair baking contests, Marjorie Johnson is the queen. She has won more than 2,447 ribbons and has appeared on both national and local TV. This blue ribbon recipe from the Minnesota State Fair has won many competitions. It makes two moist coffee cakes, one for you and one to give to a neighbor. In addition to 1,600,000 visitors, the twenty-day fair in St. Paul attracts 14,000 exhibitors who vie for the $600,000 in cash prizes at its many contests, which include judged quilts, crafts, rugs, food, and livestock. Family-style dining halls accommodate hungry fairgoers, who enjoy more than 450 different kinds of foods, including 40 different items served on sticks. Eighty artists perform on the six stages, as do the Lipizzaner Stallions. And if you're inspired to consider a new look, the cyberimage haircolor booth will show you how you'd look as a blonde or a redhead.

BATTER
- ¾ cup (1½ sticks) butter, softened
- 1½ cups granulated sugar
- 1 teaspoon vanilla extract
- 4 eggs
- 3 cups all-purpose flour
- 1½ teaspoons baking powder
- 1½ teaspoons baking soda
- ½ teaspoon salt
- 1½ cups sour cream

STREUSEL
- 2 tablespoons butter, melted
- ½ cup packed light brown sugar
- 2 tablespoons all-purpose flour
- ¼ cup sweetened flaked coconut
- ½ cup (2 ounces) sliced almonds or chopped nuts

GLAZE
- ½ cup sifted confectioners' sugar
- ¼ teaspoon almond or vanilla extract
- 1 to 3 teaspoons milk

MILTON DAIRY COMPANY'S 31st ANNUAL ORNAMENTAL BUTTER EXHIBIT DISPLAYED IN THE ONLY REVOLVING REFRIGERATOR IN THE UNITED STATES MINNESOTA STATE FAIR ~ SAINT PAUL & MINNEAPOLIS ~ SEPTEMBER 5-12 1925

Heat the oven to 350°F. Grease and flour two 8- or 9-inch cake pans.

To make the batter: Combine the butter, sugar, and vanilla in a large bowl and cream with an electric mixer. Add the eggs, one at a time, beating well after each addition. Combine the flour, baking powder, baking soda, and salt in a medium bowl and stir with a whisk to blend. On low speed or by hand, add the dry ingredients to the wet ingredients alternately with the sour cream, beginning and ending with the flour mixture. Spoon one-fourth of the batter into each prepared pan.

To make the streusel: Combine all the ingredients in a small bowl and mix with a fork. Sprinkle one-fourth of the mixture over the batter in each pan. Spoon the remaining batter equally into the 2 pans. Sprinkle the top of each with an equal amount of the remaining streusel.

Bake for 30 to 35 minutes, or until a toothpick inserted in the center comes out clean and the tops of the cakes feel firm to the touch.

Remove the cakes from the oven and let them rest for 10 minutes. Run a sharp knife around the edges and remove from the pans by gently inverting each one onto a flat dinner plate, covering it with a wire rack, and then carefully flipping it right-side up to cool on the rack.

To make the glaze: Combine all the ingredients in a small bowl and stir with a spoon until smooth. Drizzle over the tops of the cooled cakes.

Makes 2 coffee cakes; each serves 6 to 8

Cajun Smothered Venison Steak

For his skill in cooking venison, Calvin Vowell won third place in the Wild Game Crock-Pot Cooking Competition at the South Mississippi Fair. He recommends serving his dish over steamed rice or grits. In addition to its cook-off events, the fair in Laurel, which begins on the third Monday of October, draws approximately 50,000 people to its extensive livestock exhibitions and shows, carnival rides, and live entertainment.

2	pounds venison steak
	Salt, freshly ground black pepper, and cayenne pepper to taste
¼	cup vegetable oil
1	tablespoon all-purpose flour
1	onion, chopped
1	red or green bell pepper, seeded and chopped
One	14½-ounce can diced tomatoes
Two	14½-ounce cans beef broth
1	or 2 cups hot water

Season the venison with salt, pepper, and cayenne. Heat the oil in a heavy skillet over medium heat, add the venison, and brown for 3 minutes on each side. Drain on paper towels and transfer to a slow cooker. Add the flour to the skillet and cook, stirring constantly, for 4 minutes, or until it turns brown. Add the onion and bell pepper and cook for 1 minute. Add the tomatoes and beef broth, increase the heat to medium-high, and bring to a boil, stirring constantly, until a smooth gravy forms. Gradually add 1 cup of the hot water, stirring constantly. If the gravy is thick, add up to 1 more cup of hot water, to make the gravy very thin. Pour the gravy over the venison in the slow cooker. Cover and cook on low for 6 hours or on high for about 3 hours, until the venison is tender.

Serves 6 to 8

PEARL RIVER COUNTY

Fair

& LIVESTOCK SHOW

POPLARVILLE
FAIRGROUNDS
SEPT. 25 - 30

KIDDIE'S DAY - FRIDAY FROM 8 A.M. TO 6 P.M.
REDUCED RIDE PRICES - 3 FOR $1.00
DRAWING SATURDAY AT 10 P.M. FOR 2 BICYCLES
COMPLIMENTS OF MISSISSIPPI DELTA SHOWS

MISSISSIPPI DELTA SHOWS
ON THE MIDWAY

STONE COUNTY
LIVESTOCK SHOW &

FAIR

WIGGINS
FAIRGROUNDS
OCT. 4 - 7

KID'S DAY FRIDAY FROM 11 A.M. TO 6 P.M.
REDUCED RIDE PRICES - 3 FOR $1.00

MISSISSIPPI DELTA SHOWS
ON THE MIDWAY

Catfish Wraps

First place in the Missouri Conservation Agents Association Cook-Off at the Missouri State Fair went to Sarah Keyte of Clinton. The contest promotes the cooking of wild meat or fish, and has been part of the fair competitions since 1998. The ten-day fair in Sedalia boasts that it displays catfish as big as a five-year-old child, along with a full schedule of events and activities including a carnival and midway, acrobats, musicians, livestock, quilts, wedding gowns and cakes, chainsaw sculptures, a queen pageant, and truck and tractor pulls.

1	small catfish, about 1½ pounds
One	12-ounce bottle lemon pepper marinade
1	tablespoon butter or olive oil
One	11-ounce can whole-kernel corn, drained
1	yellow bell pepper, seeded and finely chopped
1	green bell pepper, seeded and finely chopped
½	cup finely chopped green onions, including green parts
1	large portobello mushroom (about 6 ounces), finely chopped
	Salt and freshly ground black pepper to taste
One	1-pound package spring roll wrappers
1	egg beaten with 3 tablespoons water, for egg wash
	Vegetable oil for deep-frying

Place the fish in a shallow baking dish, cover with the marinade, turn to coat evenly, cover with plastic wrap, and refrigerate for at least 1 hour or up to 4 hours.

Build a medium-hot fire in a charcoal grill or preheat a gas grill to 375°F. Lightly oil the grate. Remove the fish from the marinade, place it on the grill, and cook for about 4 minutes. Turn gently and cook for another 3 or 4 minutes on the second side, or until it flakes easily and

is opaque throughout. Transfer the fish to a platter and set aside.

Melt the butter or heat the olive oil in a skillet over medium heat. Add the corn, bell peppers, onions, and mushroom and sauté, stirring occasionally,

continued

DON'T MISS THIS

1953

MISSOURI STATE FAIR

51st ANNUAL

► COME THRU THE GATE FOR

9 *Wonderful* **Days & Nights**

FRIDAY — AUGUST 21
WATER CARNIVAL
SATURDAY — AUGUST 22
WATER CARNIVAL   MOTORCYCLE RACES
AUT SWENSON'S THRILLCADE   FIREWORKS
SUNDAY — AUGUST 23
WATER CARNIVAL   BIG CAR AUTO RACES
TOURNAMENT OF THRILLS
HORSE SHOW   FIREWORKS
MONDAY — AUGUST 24
WATER CARNIVAL   HORSE SHOW
GRAND CIRCUIT HARNESS RACES   FIREWORKS
TUESDAY — AUGUST 25
WATER CARNIVAL   HORSE SHOW
GRAND CIRCUIT HARNESS RACES   FIREWORKS
STAGE SHOW AND MUSICAL REVUE
WEDNESDAY — AUGUST 26
WATER SHOW   HORSE SHOW   FIREWORKS
GRAND CIRCUIT HARNESS RACES
STAGE SHOW AND MUSICAL REVUE
THURSDAY — AUGUST 27
GRAND CIRCUIT HARNESS RACES   HORSE SHOW
PROFESSIONAL WRESTLING   FIREWORKS
STAGE SHOW AND MUSICAL REVUE
FRIDAY — AUGUST 28
GRAND CIRCUIT HARNESS RACES   HORSE SHOW
STAGE SHOW AND MUSICAL REVUE
AMATEUR CONTEST   FIREWORKS
SATURDAY — AUGUST 29
BIG CAR AUTO RACES   PROFESSIONAL WRESTLING
STAGE SHOW AND MUSICAL REVUE   FIREWORKS
SUNDAY — AUGUST 30
STOCK CAR RACES   FIREWORKS
STAGE SHOW AND MUSICAL REVUE

The program of the 1953 Missouri State
Fair is chock full of glittering, fast and ex-
citing entertainment. There will be plenty
of attractions for every member of the
family—Plan now to attend several days.

AUGUST 22 thru 30
SEDALIA

MISSOURI ★ STATE FAIR

for about 5 minutes, or until tender. Remove from the heat and season with salt and pepper. Remove the skin and bones and shred the fish. Combine with the sautéed vegetables and stir to blend. Lay 1 spring roll wrapper out on the counter with one of the points facing you. Cover the other wrappers with a damp cloth. Spoon about ¼ cup of the mixture in a row across the wrapper just below the left- and right-hand corners. Bring the corner facing you up over the filling and roll halfway. Brush the uncovered edges with egg wash, fold in the side corners burrito-style, and roll up as tightly as possible. Repeat until all the wrappers are filled.

Heat 3 inches of the vegetable oil in a heavy pot or deep-fat fryer to 350°F and cook the wraps, 4 at a time, turning several times, for 5 minutes, or until lightly browned. Remove with a slotted spoon and drain on paper towels.

Makes 10 wraps

Variation: Marinate 4 catfish fillets, 3 to 5 ounces each, for at least 1 hour or up to 4 hours. Drain and bake in a preheated 400°F oven for 6 to 8 minutes.

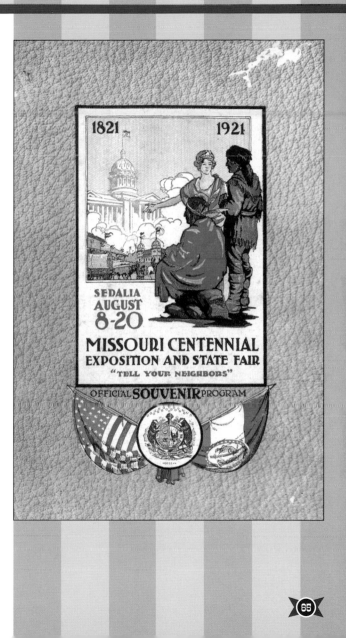

Beef Roll-Ups

FINE ARTS BUILDING   NO. MONT. STATE FAIR, GT. FALLS

This quick-and-easy recipe from Alma Winberry won first place in the Montana Beef Cook-Off, sponsored by the Montana Cattlewomen, at the Montana State Fair. She recommends serving it with spicy rice. Held in Great Falls from late July to early August, the fair offers numerous cooking competitions, carnival rides, free national and local entertainment, creative and culinary arts exhibitions, clog dancing, circus acts, a petting zoo, pig races, a look at Big Edd (the world's largest steer) and lots of other livestock, plus a special treat: deep-fried Twinkies.

6	teaspoons vegetable oil
8	to 10 white corn tortillas
1	onion, finely chopped
2	cloves garlic, minced
½	cup green chile salsa
2	cups shredded or chopped cooked pot roast
1	cup (4 ounces) shredded pepper Jack cheese
	Sour cream and/or guacamole for serving (optional)

Heat the oven to 350°F. Heat 2 teaspoons of the oil in a skillet over medium heat and fry one of the tortillas, turning after about 1 minute, until lightly cooked on both sides. Put on paper towels and set aside on a platter. Repeat with the remaining tortillas, using more oil as necessary. Add the onion and garlic to the skillet along with 2 teaspoons more oil, if necessary, and sauté for 3 minutes, or until the onion is soft.

Add the salsa and meat and heat for 3 minutes longer, stirring frequently.

Sprinkle several tablespoons of cheese on each tortilla, spoon about ¼ cup of the meat mixture on top, roll up, and place seam-side down in an 8-by-10-inch baking dish. Bake for 10 minutes, or until the cheese is completely melted. Serve topped with sour cream and/or guacamole, if desired.

Serves 4 to 8

Variation: Heat the tortillas in a preheated 300°F oven for about 5 minutes instead of frying them in oil.

Note: To have meat for this recipe, cook a pot roast weighing about 3 pounds in a slow cooker, covered with water or beef broth, along with a few carrots and an onion, for about 6 to 8 hours on low. Or, brown the meat in 1 tablespoon olive oil in a Dutch oven, cover with liquid, and simmer (covered) on the stove top or bake in a 300°F oven for several hours, or until tender.

Creamy Cheesecake

MEET ME AT PERKINS COUNTY FAIR GRANT, NEBR. AUGUST 28 to 31, 1936

With this recipe, Lisa Culbertson of Lincoln won the top prize for cheesecake at the Nebraska State Fair. Tracing its history back to 1868, the eleven-day fair, which runs from late August to early September, has taken place at the Lancaster County Fairgrounds in Lincoln since 1901. The long list of events includes a cat show, a dog show, a celebrity cattle show, chainsaw carving competitions, horse and pig racing, an antique car show, a butter sculpture, the World Grilled Cheese Eating Championship, and the Greater Omaha Barbeque Society Cook-Off.

To make the crust: Heat the oven to 325°F. Put 1 tablespoon of the butter in a 10-inch round springform pan and melt it in the oven. Remove the pan from the oven and swirl the butter around so it evenly coats the bottom of the pan. Melt the remaining 5 tablespoons of butter in a small saucepan. Add the crumbs and sugar and toss with a fork until evenly moistened. Pat the crumb mixture into the bottom of the pan to form an even crust. Bake for 10 minutes, or until

CRUST

6	tablespoons butter
1	cup graham cracker crumbs
1	tablespoon sugar

CREAM CHEESE FILLING

5	eggs
1½	cups sugar
Three 8-ounce packages cream cheese, softened	
1½	teaspoons vanilla extract
¼	cup sour cream
1	teaspoon fresh lemon juice
⅛	teaspoon salt

TOPPING

¼	cup sugar
½	teaspoon vanilla extract
½	cup sour cream

the crumbs are just beginning to brown. Remove from the oven and cool on a wire rack.

To make the filling: Beat the eggs with an electric mixer on medium speed for about 3 minutes, or

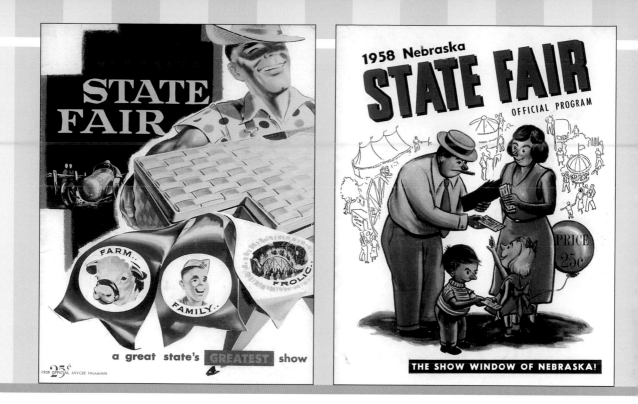

until they are very frothy and light. Add the sugar and beat 1 minute more. Add the cream cheese in chunks, about one-fourth of a package at a time, and beat until smooth. Add the vanilla, sour cream, lemon juice, and salt and beat 10 minutes more, or until the filling is very smooth and light. (Reduce the mixer speed as necessary to keep the mixture from splashing out, but do beat it for the entire 10 minutes, so the cheesecake won't be lumpy.) Pour the batter on top of the baked crust. Bake for 1½ hours, or until firmly set. (It should not jiggle when you gently move the pan from side to side.)

To make the topping: Combine all the ingredients in a bowl and whisk until smooth. Spread the topping on the warm cheesecake and bake for 10 minutes to set it slightly.

Remove the cheesecake from the oven and let it cool completely on a wire rack. Refrigerate for 4 to 6 hours or overnight. Run a sharp knife around the edges of the cake and remove the sides of the pan. Cut into wedges. (If the cheesecake is sticky, run the knife under hot water and dry it before each cut, or use a piece of dental floss to cut the wedges.)

Makes one 10-inch cheesecake; serves 10 to 12

Grilled Salsa

Roy Rudebusch of Reno created this prizewinning entry in the "My Favorite Salsa" competition at the Nevada State Fair in Reno. Grilling the vegetables mellows and deepens their flavors. The five-day fair, held in late August, was first organized in 1874. In addition to extensive livestock and agricultural displays, it features a queen and her court, pony rides, a birds-of-prey show, dirt-track auto racing, a demolition derby, table setting and pie baking contests, and a chance for the best harmonica player in Nevada to be heard.

2	pounds plum tomatoes (about 14), halved and seeded
1	Anaheim chile, halved and seeded
1	jalapeño chile, halved and seeded
1	head garlic, peeled and separated into cloves
1	small red onion, thickly sliced
	Olive oil for coating
½	teaspoon salt
	Freshly ground black pepper to taste
¼	cup fresh lime juice
⅓	cup chopped fresh cilantro

Build a medium fire in a charcoal grill, or heat a gas grill to 350°F. Put the tomatoes, chiles, garlic, and onion in a bowl and coat lightly with oil. Oil the grill grate or a vegetable basket. Arrange the vegetables on the grate or in the basket and grill, turning several times, for 10 minutes, or until the tomatoes and chiles start to char and the garlic and onion are very soft. (Or, bake the vegetables in a preheated 425°F oven for about 20 minutes, or until very soft.) Transfer the vegetables to a cutting board and let cool. Skin and stem the tomatoes and chiles. Chop the vegetables to the consistency you prefer for salsa. Transfer to a bowl and add the salt, pepper, lime juice, and cilantro. Serve immediately, or refrigerate for up to 24 hours.

Makes about 4 cups

Rosy Spiced Crab Apples

Cynthia Van Hazinga won a blue ribbon in the 4-H division at the Hillsborough County Agricultural Fair in New Boston, using crab apples from the enormous tree on her family farm, where apples have been grown for export since 1800. The fair began in 1957 to showcase local agriculture, and offers plenty of down-home fun: a giant pumpkin weigh-off, a woodsmen's contest, horseshoe pitching competitions, a cowboy shootout, and lots of entertainment, including stage shows and high-school band concerts.

4	cups sugar
3	cups cider vinegar
1	cup water
4	pounds unpeeled, unblemished, well-formed crab apples, stems intact
1	tablespoon cloves
1	tablespoon allspice berries
3	cinnamon sticks, broken into halves

Combine the sugar, vinegar, and water in a nonreactive kettle and bring to a boil over medium-high heat, stirring until the sugar is completely dissolved. Turn off the heat, add the crab apples, and let sit overnight.

Using a slotted spoon, transfer the crab apples to 6 hot, sterilized 1-pint wide-mouth canning jars. Divide the cloves and allspice berries evenly among the jars and put 1 cinnamon stick half in each jar. Bring the syrup in the kettle to a boil over medium-high heat, reduce the heat to medium, and simmer, stirring occasionally, for 20 to 30 minutes, or until the syrup thickens to the consistency of honey. Pour the syrup over the crab apples, leaving ½-inch headspace. Seal with hot, sterilized new lids and rings, and process in a boiling-water bath for 10 minutes. Store in a cool, dark place.

Makes 6 pints

STATE FAIR

PLYMOUTH, NEW HAMPSHIRE

Premium List — Advance Program

AUGUST 23, 24, 25, 26, 1962

DAY AND NIGHT

NEW HAMPSHIRE *State Parks*

FOR A

VACATION

Apple-Carrot Muffins

First place in the Youth category (under twelve) at the Warren County Farmers' Fair in Belvidere went to Julianna Hothouse for these hearty muffins with a crunchy, sweet topping. The fair has a colorful history. Organized in 1859, it attracted 6,000 visitors in its first year. Despite the depression of the 1870s, the event continued on until 1882, when it was discontinued because of public drunkenness and general rowdiness. It was revived in 1890 as the Farmers' Picnic. In 1910, 40,000 fairgoers gathered to see presidential candidate Woodrow Wilson, and in 1935 the National Bank of Blairstown was robbed while everyone was at the fair. Since 1937, the fair has been held at its present location. In addition to livestock exhibitions, the fair offers hot-air balloon rides, a mud bog competition, and a flower show.

1	large Granny Smith apple, quartered and cored
3	carrots, peeled
3	egg whites, lightly beaten
2	tablespoons canola oil
¼	cup unsweetened applesauce
½	cup packed dark brown sugar
1	teaspoon vanilla extract
¾	cup all-purpose flour
1½	teaspoons baking soda
1½	teaspoons baking powder
1	teaspoon ground cinnamon
½	teaspoon ground nutmeg
¼	teaspoon ground cloves
¼	teaspoon salt
⅓	cup quick-cooking rolled oats
⅔	cup dark or golden raisins
½	cup Grape-Nuts cereal

CRUMB TOPPING

⅔	cup packed light brown sugar
1	teaspoon ground cinnamon
½	cup all-purpose flour
¼	teaspoon nutmeg
¼	cup quick-cooking rolled oats
6	tablespoons cold butter, cut into bits

Heat the oven to 350°F. Spray or grease 12 muffin cups, or fit them with paper liners.

Shred the apple and carrots using the large holes of a box grater. Combine the apple, carrots, egg whites, oil, applesauce, brown sugar, and vanilla in a large bowl. Combine the flour, baking soda, baking powder, cinnamon, nutmeg, cloves, and salt in a medium bowl and stir with a whisk to blend. Stir the dry ingredients into the apple mixture. Add the oats, raisins, and cereal and stir until evenly moistened. Spoon the batter into the prepared muffin cups, filling each one about two-thirds full.

To make the topping: Combine the brown sugar, cinnamon, flour, nutmeg, and oats in a medium bowl and stir with a whisk to blend. Using a pastry blender or your fingertips, cut or rub in the butter until the mixture is very fine. Cover the top of the muffins with a generous amount of the topping.

Bake for 30 minutes, or until a toothpick inserted in the center of the muffins comes out clean. Let cool in the pan for 5 minutes, then unmold onto a wire rack.

Makes 12 muffins

Korean Oven-Roasted Turkey SPAM Stir-Fry

Michael S. Yang, the first place winner in the Best SPAM Recipe competition at the New Mexico State Fair, created a quick supper dish that can be enhanced by using a little minced ginger, if you wish, as a spicy garnish. The seventeen-day fair, located in Albuquerque, is held in September. The area's first fair was a territorial event organized in 1881 (New Mexico became a state in 1912). The fair has been held every year on its present site since 1938. It celebrates the state's cultural diversity and local agriculture, with livestock, arts and crafts, rides, games, and food exhibitions on 236 acres.

7	tablespoons soy sauce, or to taste
6	tablespoons packed light brown sugar
One	12-ounce can Oven-Roasted Turkey SPAM
1/4	cup all-purpose flour
1/4	cup cornstarch
3	tablespoons sesame seeds
	Olive oil for frying
1	pound snow peas, strings removed
1	red bell pepper, seeded and sliced
3	cups hot cooked white or brown rice for serving
1/4	cup slivered almonds
2	teaspoons minced fresh ginger (optional)

Combine the soy sauce and brown sugar in a flat baking dish and stir with a whisk until smooth. Cut the SPAM into 1/4-inch-thick slices and arrange them in a single layer on top of the marinade in the dish. Turn to coat both sides with marinade and let sit for 5 to 10 minutes.

Combine the flour, cornstarch, and sesame seeds in a shallow bowl and blend with a fork. Heat 1/4 inch of olive oil in a large skillet over medium-high heat. Remove the SPAM slices from the marinade and coat on both sides with the flour mixture. Fry in the hot oil for about 2 minutes per side, or until lightly browned. Transfer to paper towels

to drain. Drain all but 1 to 2 tablespoons oil from the pan. Stir-fry the snow peas and bell pepper over medium-high heat for about 1 minute, or until crisp-tender. Serve the SPAM and vegetables over the rice, sprinkled with almonds, and ginger, if desired.

Serves 4 to 6

Governor Davis Apple Pie

The New York State Fair in Syracuse takes its apple pie contests seriously, and winning entries feature delicious combinations of ingredients. Deborah Strong won the category with this pie, which honors a former Vermont governor. Running for twelve days from late August to early September, the fair dates back to 1846 and has been held almost continuously. It's one of the state's largest extravaganzas, offering a circus, free concerts, demonstrations of chain-saw artistry, living statues, a sand sculpture, flower shows, antique tractors and autos, extensive livestock exhibitions and competitions, and dozens of baking and cooking contests.

To make the pie pastry: Combine the flour, salt, baking powder, and sugar in a food processor and pulse to blend. Add the shortening and butter and pulse until the mixture is crumbly. Combine the vinegar, ½ cup of the water, and the egg in a small bowl and beat until smooth. Add the vinegar mixture to the dry ingredients

continued

PIE PASTRY

3	cups all-purpose flour
1	teaspoon salt
1	teaspoon baking powder
2	teaspoons sugar
½	cup shortening (preferably nonhydrogenated)
½	cup (1 stick) cold butter, cut into bits
½	teaspoon apple cider vinegar
½	to ¾ cup water
1	egg
6	to 8 apples, peeled, cored, and sliced
¾	cup granulated sugar
¼	cup packed light brown sugar
1	teaspoon ground cinnamon
	Pinch freshly grated nutmeg
	Pinch dried sage
3	tablespoons all-purpose flour
½	teaspoon salt
2	tablespoons maple syrup
1	tablespoon butter, cut into bits
1	teaspoon heavy (whipping) cream

Souvenir
Afton Fair 1909

Buy WATCHES and JEWELRY of
LESLIE & CARL,
Send for CATALOG   DEPOSIT, N. Y.

Souvenir
Afton Fair 1909

Buy WATCHES and JEWELRY of
LESLIE & CARL,
Send for CATALOG   DEPOSIT, N. Y.

Souvenir
Afton Fair 1909

Buy WATCHES and JEWELRY of
LESLIE & CARL,
Send for CATALOG   DEPOSIT, N. Y.

OFFICIAL
PROGRAM

SOUVENIR
NEW YORK
STATE FAIR
SYRACUSE

VISIT
BAVARIAN
BEER
GARDEN
NEW YORK STATE FAIR
1938

N.Y. STATE FAIR
Syracuse.

INTERIOR OF THE CATTLE BUILDING, NEW YORK STATE FAIR,
SYRACUSE, N. Y.

DIVING HORSES SYRACUSE FAIR,
SYRACUSE, N.Y.

32191

Pub. by Ralph Finney, Times Square Station, N. Y. City.

and pulse several times, mixing just until the dough begins to form a ball (add a little more water, if necessary). Divide in half and flatten each piece slightly with the heel of your hand. Wrap in plastic wrap and refrigerate for at least 1 hour or up to 4 hours.

Heat the oven to 400°F. Roll out one of the balls into a 12-inch round and fit it into a 10-inch pie pan. Add a layer of apples. Combine the sugars, cinnamon, nutmeg, sage, flour, and salt in a small bowl and mix with a fork. Sprinkle some of the mixture over the apples. Continue layering

the apples and dry mixture until the pan is full, ending with the dry mixture. Drizzle the maple syrup over the apples and dot with butter. Roll out the remaining ball of dough into a 12-inch round and fit it on top. Flute the crust and cut slits in the top. Brush with the cream.

Bake for 15 minutes. Lower the oven temperature to 350°F and bake for 45 to 50 minutes longer, or until the top is lightly browned. Let cool on a wire rack.

Makes one 10-inch pie; serves 8

Roasted Chicken Salad with Honey-Pecan Balsamic Dressing

The North Carolina State Fair holds a number of cooking contests, among them the North Carolina Pecan Association's Pecan Recipe Competition. Denise Walker of Cary won a blue ribbon and $100 for this recipe. One of the country's oldest fairs, North Carolina's was first held in 1853. Today, it stretches through ten days in mid-October, drawing some 800,000 people and offering the state's best livestock along with inductees to the Livestock Hall of Fame, presentations on bees and honey making, a demolition derby, and hundreds of exhibitions and demonstrations, including the lost art of tobacco auctioneering.

To make the glazed pecans: Heat the oven to 300°F. Combine the sugar, water, and maple syrup in a small bowl. Add the pecans and toss to coat. Spread the pecans on a baking sheet and toast in the oven for about 10 minutes, or until

GLAZED PECANS

¾	cup sifted confectioners' sugar
2	tablespoons water
⅛	teaspoon maple syrup
1	cup (4 ounces) pecans

HONEY-PECAN BALSAMIC DRESSING

4	teaspoons balsamic vinegar
½	cup olive oil
½	cup honey
½	teaspoon garlic powder
½	teaspoon onion powder
1	teaspoon maple syrup
½	teaspoon Dijon mustard
¼	cup chopped toasted pecans (see Note)
3	chicken breast halves, roasted
12	ounces mixed salad greens (iceberg, romaine, red cabbage, etc.)
2	Granny Smith apples, peeled, cored, and sliced

THE BIG GASTON COUNTY FAIR
⊙ GASTONIA, N.C. OCT. 8-12

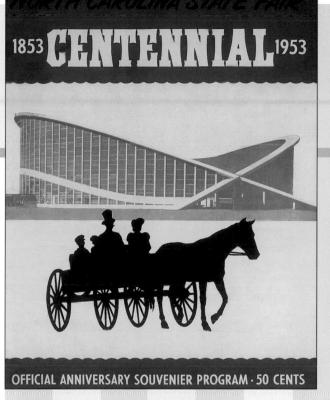

NORTH CAROLINA STATE FAIR

1853 **CENTENNIAL** 1953

OFFICIAL ANNIVERSARY SOUVENIER PROGRAM · 50 CENTS

fragrant. Remove from the oven and let cool for 10 minutes, or until the glaze is set.

To make the dressing: Combine the vinegar, olive oil, and honey in a small bowl and blend with a whisk. Whisk in the garlic powder, onion powder, maple syrup, and mustard. Add the chopped pecans and mix well. Set aside.

Remove the skin and bones from the chicken and shred the chicken. Divide the salad greens among 3 or 4 plates and put equal amounts of chicken on each serving. Arrange the apple slices on top of the chicken. Drizzle the dressing over the salads and garnish with the glazed pecans.

Serves 3 to 4

Note: To toast the pecans, spread them in a single layer in a baking pan and bake in a preheated 300°F oven for about 10 minutes, or until fragrant. Watch carefully that they don't burn.

STUCKEY'S
fine pecan CANDIES
MADE FROM THE SOUTH'S FINEST PECANS

Susan's Fettuccine

Susan Sorvaag won the Dakota Growers Pasta Cooking Contest at the Red River Valley Fair in West Fargo with this versatile main dish. If you're low on zucchini and broccoli, she recommends using any other vegetables you have on hand in their place. Held for nine days in mid-June, the fair attracts nationally known entertainers and offers extreme racing, sprint races, livestock and arts and crafts shows, and sets aside special days for senior citizens and teens. It also has a pioneer village that gives visitors a glimpse of early settlers' lives.

1	pound dried fettuccine pasta
2	tablespoons olive oil
1	onion, chopped
5	ounces mushrooms, sliced
1	zucchini, sliced
1	cup broccoli florets, cut into small pieces
10	tablespoons butter, cut into bits
¾	cup heavy (whipping) cream
¾	cup (3 ounces) grated Parmesan cheese

In a large pot of salted boiling water, cook the fettuccine until al dente, about 8 minutes. While the pasta cooks, heat the olive oil in a large skillet over medium heat and sauté the onion, mushrooms, zucchini, and broccoli for 5 minutes, or until crisp-tender. Drain the fettuccine and toss with the butter, cream, and Parmesan cheese. Serve the pasta hot, with the sautéed vegetables on the side or on top.

Serves 4

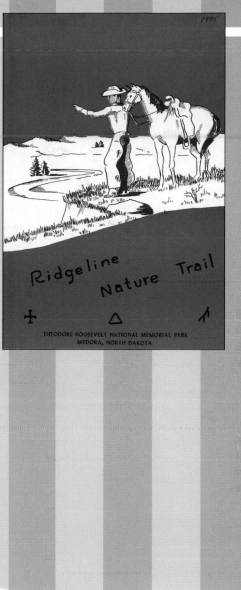

Don's Peach Pie

The President's Jackpot Baking Contest at the Montgomery County Fair in Dayton follows the old fair tradition of asking all the contestants to bake the same recipe. Entries are judged and the winning pie is immediately auctioned. This pie was first created by fair president Don Michael's wife, Carol. The fair, which can trace its history back to the cattle and stock exhibitions of the 1850s, has several claims to fame beyond this fine pie. Its mid-nineteenth-century three-story Round House exhibition hall has earned a place on the National Register of Historic Places, and in the 1930s electric lights were installed around the race track, making this the first fair in Ohio to hold night harness racing. Special events today include motorcycle racing and a dog agility show.

Pastry for a 2-crust pie
¾ cup sugar
3 tablespoons all-purpose flour
¼ teaspoon ground nutmeg or cinnamon, plus more if needed
¼ teaspoon almond extract
Pinch of salt
8 peaches, peeled, pitted, and sliced (5 cups)
2 tablespoons butter, cut into bits

Heat the oven to 375°F. Line a 9-inch pie plate with 1 circle of pastry. Combine the sugar, flour, the ¼ teaspoon nutmeg or cinnamon, the almond extract, and salt in a small bowl and stir with a whisk to blend. Put the peaches in a large bowl, add the dry ingredients, and mix lightly. Spoon the mixture into the pie shell. Dot with the butter and add a bit of extra nutmeg or cinnamon, if desired. Top with pastry, crimp the edges, and cut vents in the top. Bake for 45 to 50 minutes, or until the crust is lightly browned and the juices are bubbling at the vents.

Makes one 9-inch pie; serves 6 to 8

Oklahoma Wagon Wheels

Teresa Evans won first place at the Oklahoma State Fair in *The Oklahoman*'s Best Homemade Cinnamon Roll Contest. She used fresh local ingredients, right down to the certified organic eggs. The ten-day fair in Oklahoma City includes a rodeo, motorcycle races, monster truck races, pony and camel rides, Indian dancers, the Royal Lipizzaner Stallions, school band competitions, an antique-tractor parade, a modeling contest, and fair treats such as chicken on a stick, fried pickles, tater twirls, and elephant ear pastries.

Put the water in a large bowl, add the yeast and honey, and stir until blended. Let sit until foamy, about 10 minutes. Add the warm milk to the yeast mixture along with the salt, butter, and eggs. Beat until smooth. Add the flours, 1 cup at a time, mixing to form a stiff dough. Turn the dough out onto a floured work surface and knead until smooth and elastic, 8 to 10 minutes. Place in an oiled bowl and turn to coat. Cover with plastic wrap and let rise in a warm place until doubled, about 1 hour.

½ cup warm (105° to 115°F) water
1 package active dry yeast
¾ cup honey
½ cup warm milk (105° to 115°F)
1 teaspoon salt
½ cup (1 stick) butter, softened
2 eggs
4 cups all-purpose flour
2 cups whole-wheat flour

PECAN TOPPING
1 cup (4 ounces) pecans
½ cup (1 stick) butter
¾ cup honey or packed light brown sugar

CINNAMON FILLING
1 cup granulated sugar or packed light brown sugar
1½ teaspoons ground cinnamon
1 to 2 tablespoons butter, softened
¾ cup (3 ounces) chopped pecans

To make the topping: Generously butter a 10-inch cast-iron skillet or a 10-inch round baking pan that is 2 inches deep. Arrange the pecans in a single layer in the pan. Melt the butter in a small saucepan over low heat, add the honey or sugar, and stir until smooth. Pour the mixture over the pecans.

Roll out the dough into a rectangle about 10 inches wide and 20 inches long, with one long side parallel to the counter.

To make the filling: Combine the sugar and cinnamon in a small bowl and stir with a fork until blended. Cover the surface of the rolled-out dough with the butter and sprinkle with the cinnamon sugar and pecans. Carefully roll the dough up tightly. Cut into ten 2-inch-thick rolls and arrange, cut-side down, in the prepared pan. Cover with a cloth and let rise in a warm place until doubled, about 45 minutes.

Heat the oven to 350°F. Bake for 30 to 40 minutes, or until the rolls are light brown and sound hollow when gently tapped. Remove from the oven and let cool in the pan for 10 minutes. Unmold the rolls onto a serving plate.

Makes 10 rolls

Bacon Cheeseburger Potato Salad

David D. Allen of Salem was a first-place winner in the Oregon Potato Commission contest at the Oregon State Fair. Baking the potatoes lends great flavor and texture to this salad. When served to teenage boys, this skillet supper will disappear in seconds. Held for eleven days from late August to early September, the fair shines the spotlight on local entertainment, and hosts the Best of Oregon Music Festival, along with livestock exhibitions, cooking and crafts competitions, and bull-riding contests. Among the hair-raising rides is the Human Slingshot, which propels riders three hundred feet into the air at ninety miles per hour.

4	russet potatoes, baked
4	slices bacon
½	pound lean ground beef
1	onion, chopped
2	tablespoons sugar
1	tablespoon all-purpose flour
½	teaspoon salt
1	teaspoon dried dill
¼	teaspoon dried thyme
½	teaspoon dried parsley
1	clove garlic, minced
½	teaspoon onion powder
½	teaspoon freshly ground black pepper
½	cup water
¼	cup cider vinegar
½	cup (2 ounces) shredded Cheddar cheese

Peel the potatoes and cut into ½-inch dice. Fry the bacon in a skillet over medium heat until crisp. Transfer to paper towels to drain. Drain the fat from the skillet. Cook the beef in the skillet over medium heat, breaking it up into small pieces. When it is no longer pink, use a slotted spoon to transfer it to a plate. Add the onion to the pan and cook for 5 minutes, or until soft.

Stir in the sugar, flour, salt, dill, thyme, parsley, garlic, onion powder, and pepper. Cook, stirring, for about 2 minutes, or until the flour starts to brown. Add the water and vinegar and simmer

Fruit Pyramid in Pavillion, Horticultural Section,
Oregon State Fair. SALEM, Ore.

for 2 to 3 minutes, stirring to make a smooth sauce. Crumble the bacon into the sauce and add the cooked beef. Add the potatoes and stir gently to coat with sauce. Pour into a serving dish and sprinkle with the cheese. Serve hot.

Serves 4 to 6

Variation: To reduce the fat in this dish, use turkey bacon. Add 2 teaspoons olive oil to the pan before cooking the onion. Use grated Parmesan cheese instead of Cheddar, or omit the cheese altogether.

Jim Bob's Chocolate-Molasses Cake

With this recipe, Jim Harper of Furnace won second place in the Shoo-Fly Cake and Pie Contest at the Pennsylvania Farm Show in Harrisburg. The moist sheet cake is topped off with peanut butter frosting. Since 1917, the show, held for eight days in mid-January, has offered visitors all the fun of a traditional agricultural fair—indoors (!) —in the nation's largest agricultural exposition under a roof. The events are spread out over twenty-five acres and include a rodeo, extensive livestock exhibitions and shows, a sale of champion livestock, a life-size butter sculpture, several cooking contests, and displays of farm equipment.

Heat the oven to 350°F. Grease and flour a 9-by-13-inch baking pan.

Combine the sugar, flour, cocoa, baking powder, baking soda, and salt in a large bowl and stir with a whisk to blend. Add the eggs, milk, molasses, oil, and vanilla and beat for 2 minutes. Add the water and stir it into the batter by hand. Pour the batter, which will be very thin, into the

2	cups granulated sugar
1¾	cups all-purpose flour
¾	cup unsweetened cocoa powder
1½	teaspoons baking powder
1½	teaspoons baking soda
1	teaspoon salt
2	eggs
1	cup milk
½	cup dark molasses
½	cup vegetable oil
2	teaspoons vanilla extract
1	cup boiling water

FROSTING

½	cup (1 stick) butter, softened
1	cup peanut butter
8	ounces cream cheese, softened
4	cups sifted confectioners' sugar
3	to 4 teaspoons milk

prepared pan and bake for 35 to 45 minutes, or until a toothpick inserted in the center comes out clean. Remove from the oven and let cool completely on a wire rack.

To make the frosting: Combine the butter, peanut butter, and cream cheese in a large bowl and beat until fluffy. Slowly add the confectioners' sugar, beating to form a smooth frosting. Add the milk 1 teaspoon at a time until the frosting reaches the desired spreading consistency.

Frost the cake and let it sit for 30 minutes before cutting into squares to serve.

Makes 1 sheet cake; serves 12 to 14

Variation: Omit the frosting and dust the cake with confectioners' sugar. let cool com-

Apple-Cinnamon Oatmeal Bread

In the tradition of early country fairs, all the baking contest participants at the Washington County Fair in Richmond make the same recipe, such as this bread, and the judges compare the entries to find the best. In 1967, members of the Washington County Pomona Grange decided to start an all-volunteer fair, and their efforts have grown into the state's largest agricultural event. The five days in August are packed with fun: a swine obstacle course, a motorcycle rodeo, a bunny race, a rooster-crowing contest, a woodsman contest, lawnmower races, a watermelon-seed-spitting competition, and a dung-throwing contest.

4	tablespoons butter, softened
1	cup sugar
1	cup chunky applesauce
1½	teaspoons ground cinnamon
2	packets (single-serving size) instant apple-cinnamon oatmeal
2	eggs
1½	cups all-purpose flour
1	teaspoon baking soda

Heat the oven to 350°F. Lightly grease and flour a 9-by-5-inch loaf pan.

Combine the butter and sugar in a large bowl and beat until light and fluffy. Mix in the applesauce, cinnamon, and 1 packet of oatmeal. Add the eggs, one at a time, beating well after each addition. In a medium bowl, combine the flour and baking soda and stir with a whisk to blend. Add the dry ingredients to the wet ingredients and beat just until smooth. Spoon the batter into the prepared pan, smooth the top, and sprinkle evenly with the remaining packet of oatmeal. Bake for 60 minutes, or until a toothpick inserted into the center of the loaf comes out clean. Let cool on a wire rack. When cool, unmold and serve, or wrap tightly in aluminum foil.

Makes 1 loaf; serves 8 to 10

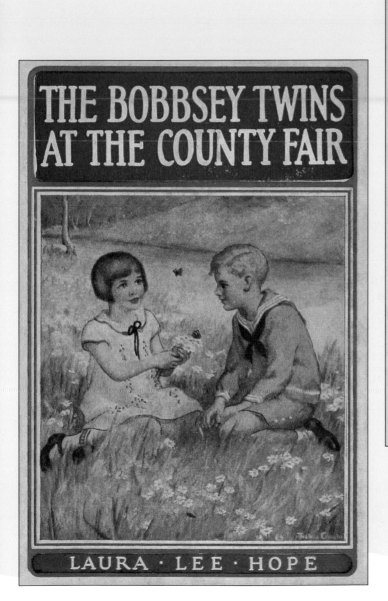

THE BOBBSEY TWINS AT THE COUNTY FAIR

LAURA · LEE · HOPE

NEWPORT
and the historic Island of
RHODE ISLAND

ANCIENT TREADMILL FERRY

On the
Scenic Route
to SAKONNET
CAPE COD
and
NEW ENGLAND'S
Greatest
Seashore Resorts

Japanese Fruitcake

Annie Lea Hiers from Cayce won a ribbon for this tasty fruitcake at the South Carolina State Fair in Columbia. Constructed of five thin layers, it makes beautiful slices, and is unrelated to the typical holiday fruitcake. Held for ten days in October, the fair began in the mid-nineteenth century and has run almost continuously except for the Civil War years: fair buildings were occupied by Confederate munitions makers in 1861, burned by Sherman's army in 1865, and rebuilt in 1869. Today's visitors can enjoy livestock, art, and flower shows; a swine costume contest; and a backhoe rodeo, along with rides, food exhibitions, and crafts.

Heat the oven to 300°F. Grease and lightly flour five 9-inch round cake pans.

Combine the butter and sugar in a large bowl and beat until light and fluffy. Combine the flour and baking powder in a medium bowl and stir with a whisk to blend. Add to the creamed mixture along with the milk and beat until smooth. Add the eggs, one at a time, beating well after each

1	cup (2 sticks) butter, softened
2	cups sugar
4	cups all-purpose flour
1	teaspoon baking powder
½	cup milk
5	eggs
1	cup raisins
1	cup chopped candied cherries (red and green)
1	cup (4 ounces) chopped pecans
1	teaspoon ground cinnamon
1	teaspoon ground cloves
1	teaspoon ground nutmeg

FILLING

	Grated zest and juice of 2 lemons
2	cups sugar
One	8-ounce can crushed pineapple
3	tablespoons cornstarch
2	cups sweetened grated coconut
1	cup boiling water

addition. Spoon about 1 cup of the batter into each of 3 of the prepared pans, reserving the remaining batter. Gently smooth the batter into a thin, even layer in each pan. Bake for 20 to 25 minutes, or just until firm; do not brown. Add the raisins, cherries, pecans, and spices to the remaining batter and divide between the remaining 2 cake pans. Bake for 25 to 30 minutes, or just until firm.

To make the filling: Combine all the ingredients in a double boiler and cook over barely simmering water, stirring frequently, for 10 minutes, or until thick. Let the filling cool slightly.

Stack the cake in this order, spreading about ½ cup of the warm filling evenly between the layers with a knife: plain layer, fruited layer, plain layer, fruited layer, plain layer. Spread the remaining filling on top of the cake. Let the cake sit for 30 minutes before serving. To serve, cut into thin slices with a sharp knife and carefully place the slices on dessert plates, keeping the layers intact.

Makes one 9-inch cake; serves 12 to 14

Variation: If you're not a fan of candied cherries, substitute dried cranberries, dried cherries, or diced dried apricots.

Pumpkin Streusel Sweet Rolls

Linda Tom won a blue ribbon at the Sioux Empire Fair in Sioux Falls with these lovely-looking and great-tasting rolls. She won a second blue ribbon and $120 when she entered the recipe in the Fleischmann's Yeast Dynamic Duo Baking Contest. Serve warm from the oven for a special treat. The largest fair in the state, the six-day event dates back to 1939. It offers on-grounds camping facilities with full hook-ups, a plus for anyone who wants to spend several days seeing everything, including the bingo tent; extensive flower and horticultural displays; a display of scroll sawing; local, regional, and national talent shows; and extreme carnival rides.

Combine 1½ cups of the flour, the sugar, lemon zest, salt, and yeast in a large mixing bowl and stir with a whisk to blend. Combine the milk, pumpkin, and butter in a saucepan and heat over medium-low heat, stirring frequently, until the butter melts and the mixture is very warm (120° to 130°F), 5 to 7 minutes. Add the pumpkin mixture to the flour mixture and blend at low speed until

4¾	to 5¾ cups all-purpose flour
½	cup granulated sugar
2	teaspoons grated lemon zest
1½	teaspoons salt
1	package active dry yeast
1¼	cups milk
1	cup canned pumpkin
½	cup (1 stick) butter

CRUMB TOPPING

1½	cups all-purpose flour
1	cup firmly packed light brown sugar
1	teaspoon ground cinnamon
½	teaspoon ground allspice
¾	cup (1½ sticks) butter, cut into bits
½	cup (2 ounces) chopped nuts

GLAZE

1	cup sifted confectioners' sugar
½	teaspoon vanilla extract
3	to 4 teaspoons milk

moistened. Beat for 3 minutes at medium speed. By hand, stir in an additional 2½ to 3 cups of flour until the dough pulls cleanly away from the sides of the bowl. Transfer the dough to a floured surface and gradually knead in ¾ to 1¼ cups of flour until the dough is smooth and elastic, 5 to 8 minutes. Place the dough in a greased bowl, turn to grease it evenly, and cover with plastic wrap. Let rise in a warm place until doubled in size, about 1 hour.

To make the topping: Combine the flour, brown sugar, cinnamon, and allspice in a mixing bowl and stir with a whisk to blend. Cut or rub in the butter using a pastry blender or your fingertips. Set the nuts aside.

Grease a 10-by-15-inch baking pan. Punch the dough down several times to remove all the air bubbles. Roll out on the lightly floured surface into a 15-by-20-inch rectangle. Spoon 2½ cups crumb topping evenly over the dough. Sprinkle on the nuts. Starting with a long side, roll up tightly, jelly-roll style, pressing the edges to seal. Cut into twenty 1-inch-thick slices. Place each slice, cut-side down, in the prepared pan. Cover with a cloth and let rise in a warm place until doubled, about 45 minutes.

Heat the oven to 350°F. Uncover the dough and sprinkle the rolls with the remaining

topping. Bake for 35 to 40 minutes, or until golden brown.

To make the glaze: Blend all the ingredients together in a small bowl, adding a bit more milk if necessary for the desired consistency. Drizzle the glaze over the warm rolls.

Makes 20 rolls

Strawberry Cobbler

Connie Cobern and her family have been active in the Tennessee State Fair for more than thirty years. This recipe is one of her many blue-ribbon winners. The first fair in the state was held in 1869, and in 1891 the present-day fairground site in Nashville was first used for harness racing. Today's visitors can enjoy truck and tractor pulls, acrobats, a karaoke contest, racing pigs, demonstrations of cow milking and sorghum making, plus a flea market considered to be the best in the state and one of the top ten in the United States.

CRUST

3	cups all-purpose flour
½	teaspoon salt
1	cup butter-flavored shortening
¾	cup plus 2 tablespoons cold water
1	pound frozen whole strawberries, thawed
1½	cups sugar
1	cup water
1	tablespoon cornstarch
4	tablespoons cold butter, cut into bits

To make the crust: Combine the flour and salt in a large bowl and stir with a whisk to blend. Using a pastry blender, 2 dinner knives, or your fingertips, cut or rub in the shortening until crumbly. Add the water and stir with a fork to make a dough that can be formed into a soft ball. Divide in half. On a lightly floured board, roll out one half into a 10-by-14-inch rectangle to fit the bottom and sides of an 8-by-12-inch glass baking dish, with a 2-inch overhang all around.

Heat the oven to 350°F. Combine the strawberries, sugar, water, and cornstarch in a medium bowl and stir to blend. Spoon into the crust. Dot the filling with the butter. Roll out the top crust to a 10-by-14-inch rectangle and cut a design in it. Place the top crust on the filling, joining the bottom crust. Turn the edges under and flute the crust. Bake for 55 to 60 minutes, or until golden brown.

Makes one 8-by-12-inch cobbler; serves 10 to 12

Variations: Add ½ cup thinly sliced rhubarb to the strawberries. Substitute 1 cup (2 sticks) of butter for the shortening.

Note: Connie Cobern has compiled a book containing more than three hundred recipes for good home cooking, including more of her fair-winners. Copies of *A Lifetime Collection* are available for $18, plus $2 shipping and handling per book, from Connie Cobern, 124 Clearview Circle, Hendersonville, TN 37075.

Mushroom Moussaka

Rob Crook of Dallas won the Best of Show Award in the All-American Casseroles contest at the Texas State Fair in Dallas for this light vegetarian dish. You can count on being asked for the recipe when you serve it to guests. The three-week extravaganza, dating back to 1886, covers 277 acres, shows off 8,000 livestock entries, and brings in more than $23 million each year. Among the miles of concessions is a new treat: fried peanut butter, jelly, and banana sandwiches. Every year since 1929, the Texas-OU football game has been played at the fairgrounds Cotton Bowl stadium during the fair. Presiding over it all is the talking Big Tex, a 52-foot-tall statue that sports size-70 boots and a 75-gallon hat.

Heat the oven to 400°F. Line a large baking pan with aluminum foil and brush or spray the foil with oil. Arrange the eggplant and potato in a single layer and sprinkle with salt and pepper. Bake for 20 minutes.

1	large eggplant, cut crosswise into ¼-inch slices
1	large baking potato, cut crosswise into ¼-inch slices
	Salt and freshly ground black pepper to taste
4	tablespoons unsalted butter
1	onion, finely chopped
3	cloves garlic, minced
1	pound button mushrooms, sliced
One	14½-ounce can chopped tomatoes, drained
1	teaspoon sugar
⅓	cup all-purpose flour
2	cups milk
1	egg, slightly beaten
¼	cup grated Parmesan cheese

While the vegetables are baking, melt 2 tablespoons of the butter in a large skillet over medium heat. Add the onion and cook for 3 to 4 minutes, or until soft. Add the garlic and cook for 1 minute

continued

Fair Facts & Guide

The Official Souvenir Program of the

STATE FAIR of TEXAS

DALLAS, TEXAS

25¢ OCTOBER 4 to OCTOBER 19, 1 9 4 1

longer. Add the mushrooms and cook, stirring frequently, for 2 to 3 minutes, or until soft. Add the tomatoes, reduce the heat to medium-low, and simmer, stirring occasionally, for 8 to 10 minutes, or until the liquid in the pan is slightly reduced. Stir in the sugar and remove from the heat.

Melt the remaining 2 tablespoons of butter in a medium saucepan over low heat. Add the flour and cook, stirring constantly, for 1 minute, or until it begins to sizzle. Remove from the heat and gradually whisk in the milk. Return to medium heat and stir constantly for about 4 minutes, or until the sauce boils and thickens. Reduce the heat to medium-low and simmer for 2 minutes. Remove from the heat and let cool for 5 minutes. Add the egg and cheese, and stir until smooth.

Remove the eggplant and potatoes from the oven. Reduce the heat to 350°F.

Grease a 10-inch soufflé dish. Spoon one-third of the mushroom mixture into the dish. Cover with the potatoes and top with half of the remaining mushroom mixture. Cover with the eggplant and top with the last of the mushroom mixture. Pour on the sauce. Bake for 30 to 35 minutes, or until the edges bubble and the top is just starting to brown. Remove from the oven and let rest for 10 minutes before serving.

Serves 4 to 6

Note: Peel the eggplant and potatoes or leave them unpeeled, as you prefer. The slices "melt" into the casserole if you peel them; they remain more intact if you don't.

Five-Minute Crock-Pot Burritos

This recipe, created by Renae Woods of Ogden, takes just five minutes to assemble once the pork is cooked, which helped to make it a winner with the judges at the Utah State Fair. Serve it on a bed of black beans or Spanish rice. The fair traces its history back to the Deseret Fair in 1856. One of its early blue-ribbon winners was Brigham Young, who took home the top prize in the Best Celery exhibition. The ten-day event now attracts more than 300,000 visitors, who enjoy the butter cow sculpture, a giant slide, jugglers and magicians, a strolling organ grinder, chain-saw carving, trick roping, square dancing, horseshoe-pitching contests, numerous cook-offs, a Beef Feast, a horse show, and fireworks.

3	pounds bone-in sirloin-end pork roast
2	teaspoons Southwest seasoning
4	cups mild or medium-hot tomato salsa
Six	to eight 8-inch flour tortillas
1	cup (4 ounces) shredded Cheddar and Monterey Jack cheese blend
	Chopped fresh cilantro for garnish

Rub the pork roast with the Southwest seasoning. Pour 2 cups of the salsa into the bottom of a slow cooker, add the roast, and cover it with 1 more cup of salsa. Cover and cook on low for 6 to 8 hours, or until the meat falls from the bone. Remove the meat from the slow cooker and shred it with a fork. Place it in a medium bowl and stir in ½ cup liquid from the slow cooker.

Heat the oven to 350°F. Place the tortillas on an ovenproof platter and heat in the oven for 1 minute. Heat the broiler. Remove the tortillas from the oven, fill each with about ½ cup of the meat mixture, and roll up. Arrange them on the platter, seam-side down. Top with the remaining 1 cup salsa and the cheese, and broil 8 inches from the heat for about 3 minutes, or until the cheese is bubbly. Serve hot, garnished with the cilantro.

Serves 4 to 6

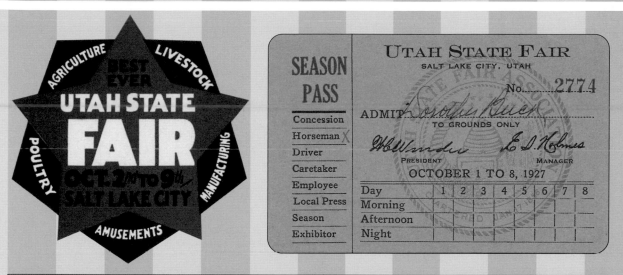

BEST EVER
UTAH STATE FAIR
OCT. 2nd TO 9th
SALT LAKE CITY

AGRICULTURE · LIVESTOCK · MANUFACTURING · POULTRY · AMUSEMENTS

SEASON PASS

Concession
Horseman X
Driver
Caretaker
Employee
Local Press
Season
Exhibitor

UTAH STATE FAIR
SALT LAKE CITY, UTAH

No. 2774

ADMIT Dorothy Buck
TO GROUNDS ONLY

W.C. Winder
PRESIDENT

E. D. Holmes
MANAGER

OCTOBER 1 TO 8, 1927

Day	1	2	3	4	5	6	7	8
Morning								
Afternoon								
Night								

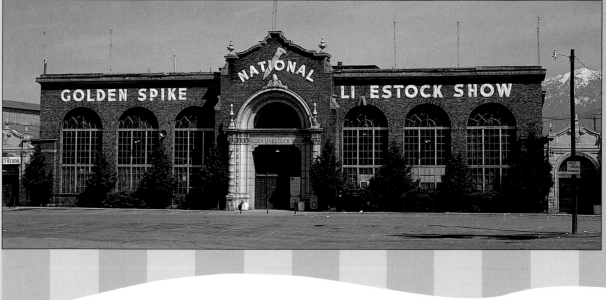

Vegetarian Stuffed-Pepper Medley

When the New England Dairy Promotion Board sponsored a recipe contest at the Champlain Valley Fair in Essex Junction to showcase their Great Cheeses of New England program, they were pleasantly surprised to receive three times the expected number of entries. After 2½ hours of tasting, the judges awarded the blue ribbon and $200 to Cambridge resident Sarah Stein for this South American–style dish. The ten-day fair, held from late August to early September, draws some 300,000 people, who come to see the two-hundred-ton sand sculpture; the food and livestock exhibitions; a crafts show; ox, horse, and antique-tractor pulls; and prizes awarded for the heaviest pumpkin, the heaviest zucchini, the longest bean pod, the tallest sunflower, and the best maple fudge.

3	large red bell peppers, halved lengthwise and seeded
2	tablespoons olive oil
1	onion, chopped
3	cloves garlic, minced
1	cup cooked red or white quinoa
½	cup peeled and diced tomato
½	cup drained canned black beans
½	cup cooked corn kernels
2	teaspoons chopped fresh cilantro
1½	teaspoons chopped fresh oregano, preferably Mexican
	Salt to taste
2	cups (8 ounces) shredded pepper Jack cheese
½	cup fresh bread crumbs

Heat the oven to 350°F. Blanch the bell peppers in a large pot of boiling water for 2 minutes; drain. Oil a baking dish just large enough to hold the peppers in a single layer (about 8 by 10 inches) and arrange the peppers, cut-side up, in the dish.

Heat the olive oil over medium heat in a medium skillet. Add the onion and garlic and

144th Annual
VERMONT State Fair
features
Rutland County Stamp Club's
Philatelic Exhibition

ANNUAL 50 FRAME STAMP
AND
POSTCARD SHOW
September 2 thru 10, 1989

COVER BY
RUTLAND COUNTY STAMP CLUB

sauté until softened, about 4 minutes. Using a slotted spoon, transfer the onion and garlic to a large bowl. Add the quinoa, tomato, beans, corn, cilantro, oregano, and salt to the pan. Add 1⅔ cups of the cheese and stir to combine. Spoon the filling into the pepper halves. Sprinkle the tops with bread crumbs and the remaining ⅓ cup cheese. Bake for 30 to 40 minutes, or until golden brown. Serve hot.

Serves 6

No. 6. The Roosevelt Bears at the County Fair
" They walked on ropes drawn good and tight
And jumped through hoops and landed right."

Championship Chili

C hef John Maxwell of Highland Springs won first place at the State Fair of Virginia for this flavorful dish, a good one to double for a large group. His original winning recipe calls for a mixture of partially cooked black beans and the beautiful maroon-and-white speckled heirloom Anasazi beans (see Variation). The following recipe uses canned pinto beans to save time. Serve it with corn bread. Fairs were being held in Richmond as early as the mid-1800s. Today's twelve-day event, which runs from late September to early October, shows off the state's agricultural character with its farm and livestock exhibition, equine yard sale, team roping, and hog-calling and rooster-crowing contests. Visitors can also enjoy fiddle, banjo, and harmonica competitions, arts and crafts displays, an antiques row, a Civil War encampment, and storytelling hours.

2	teaspoons peanut oil
1	pound diced beef (top round steak or chuck)
½	pound diced pork (sirloin roast or loin roast)
1	onion, diced
1	green bell pepper, diced
2	garlic cloves, minced
½	cup medium-hot tomato salsa
½	cup tomato paste
¼	cup dry red wine
1	whole bay leaf
1	tablespoon ground cumin
1	canned chipotle chile, minced
1	poblano chile, diced
½	cup strong black instant coffee
4	cups (32 ounces) beef broth
One	15½-ounce can pinto beans, drained
Two	15½-ounce cans diced tomatoes, drained
1	tablespoon dried oregano
½	tablespoon freshly ground black pepper
¼	cup malt vinegar

Heat the peanut oil in a large, heavy pot and brown the beef and pork over medium-high heat, stirring so they cook evenly, for about 6 minutes. Add the onion, bell pepper, and garlic and cook 4 minutes more, or until the garlic is just starting to brown. Add the salsa and tomato paste and cook for 5 minutes, stirring several times. Add the wine and cook, stirring to loosen any bits that have stuck to the bottom of the pan, for 5 minutes. Add all the remaining ingredients, reduce the heat to medium-low, and simmer for about 1 hour, or until the sauce has thickened. Remove the bay leaf before serving.

Serves 8 to 10

Variation: Soak 1 cup of black beans and 1 cup of Anasazi beans separately, overnight. Then drain and simmer separately in water to cover for 1½ hours, or until partially cooked. Drain and add to the chili for the last hour of cooking.

Chocolate Crunch Brownies

Darice Oliver and her daughter each entered this recipe in a separate division at the Skamania County Fair, and each received a blue ribbon for her efforts. Held for four days in Stevenson, in the heart of the Columbia River Gorge National Scenic Area, the fair draws some 16,000 people and is the county's largest event. It hosts a timber carnival, a parade, a talent show, cooking demonstrations, jugglers, comedians, snake handlers, and a public-speaking competition.

Heat the oven to 350°F. Grease a 9-by-13-inch baking pan. Combine the butter and sugar in a large bowl and beat until light and fluffy. Add the eggs and vanilla; beat until smooth. Stir in the cocoa, flour, and salt. Spread the mixture in the prepared pan and bake for 25 minutes, or until the brownies are firm and a toothpick inserted in the center comes out clean. Transfer the pan to a wire rack to cool for 20 minutes.

Spread the marshmallow crème over the cooled brownies. Combine the peanut butter and chocolate chips in a medium saucepan and stir

1	cup (2 sticks) butter, softened
2	cups sugar
4	eggs
2	teaspoons vanilla extract
6	tablespoons unsweetened cocoa powder
1	cup all-purpose flour
½	teaspoon salt
One	7½-ounce jar marshmallow crème
1	cup creamy peanut butter
2	cups (12 ounces) semisweet chocolate chips
3	cups crisp rice cereal

over low heat until the chocolate melts and the mixture is smooth, watching carefully so it doesn't burn. Remove from the heat and stir in the cereal. Spread the coated cereal over the marshmallow layer. Refrigerate for at least 3 hours before cutting into bars.

Makes 3 dozen bars

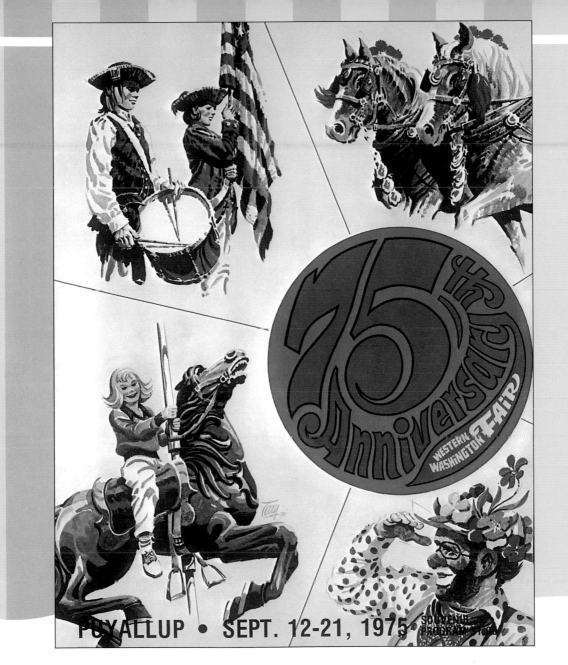

PUYALLUP • SEPT. 12-21, 1975

113

Marbled Banana Bars

The Land O'Lakes food company sponsors a number of cooking contests around the country. At one of their events at the State Fair of West Virginia in Lewisburg, Linda Clemmons and Donald Spry won top honors for these moist and beautifully marbled bars, a great snack with tea or coffee. The ten-day fair, held in mid-August, has a long history. The first fair was held in Lewisburg in 1858, before West Virginia became a state. The present family-oriented event has been running since 1924. Visitors can count on seeing the best of the region's livestock, plus hundreds of exhibitions and displays, bull riding, and traditional bluegrass music. They can also enjoy some of the world's best barbecue.

1	cup granulated sugar
½	cup (1 stick) butter, softened
1½	cups mashed ripe bananas (about 4)
1	large egg
1	teaspoon vanilla extract
1½	cups all-purpose flour
1	teaspoon baking powder
1	teaspoon baking soda
½	teaspoon salt
¼	cup unsweetened cocoa powder
	Confectioners' sugar for dusting (optional)

Heat the oven to 350°F. Grease a 9-by-13-inch baking pan. Combine the sugar and butter in a large bowl and beat with an electric mixer on medium speed, scraping the bowl several times, until light and fluffy, 1 to 2 minutes. Add the bananas, egg, and vanilla and continue beating and scraping the bowl until well mixed, 1 to 2 minutes longer. Combine the flour, baking powder, baking soda, and salt in a medium bowl and stir with a whisk to blend. Add to the banana mixture and beat on low speed for 1 to 2 minutes, scraping the bowl several times, until the batter is well mixed.

Measure out 1½ cups of the batter and drop it by spoonfuls into the prepared pan, leaving a few spaces. Add the cocoa to the remaining batter

in the bowl and beat on low speed for about 30 seconds, or until well mixed. Drop the chocolate batter by spoonfuls into the pan over and around the banana batter. Using a knife, swirl the chocolate batter through the banana batter to make a marbleized pattern. (Do not overswirl.) Bake for 20 to 25 minutes, or until a toothpick inserted in the center comes out clean. Transfer to a wire rack to cool completely in the pan. Just before serving, dust with confectioners' sugar, if desired. Cut into bars.

Makes about 36 bars

Old-Fashioned Sausages and Peppers

The winner of Usinger's Top Sausage Award in the entrée category at the Wisconsin State Fair, Rebecca Trongard of Pewaukee, took home a blue ribbon and a $100 gift certificate. Her recipe uses two skillets, which assures that the sausages cook evenly. Located just outside of Milwaukee in West Allis, the eleven-day fair was first held in 1851. It proudly displays the state's livestock in grand style, in venues such as the Fine Swine Booth and the Poultry and Rabbit Palace. Fairgoers can enjoy gardening and yo-yo demonstrations, a circus, Irish dancers, a National Clydesdale show, and exhibitions featuring local maple syrup, cranberries, honey, and potatoes. The fair food is legendary, and includes maple syrup cotton candy, bratwurst, giant brownies, cream puffs, watermelonade, and thirty microbrews.

continued

¼	cup extra-virgin olive oil
2	cloves garlic, thinly sliced
1	large red onion, cut into 2-inch chunks
2	red bell peppers, seeded and cut into 2-inch chunks
2	green bell peppers, seeded and cut into 2-inch chunks
4	hot Italian sausages
4	sweet Italian sausages
1	cup crushed canned Italian plum tomatoes
1½	cups Chianti wine
	Pinch of dried oregano
	Salt and freshly ground black pepper to taste

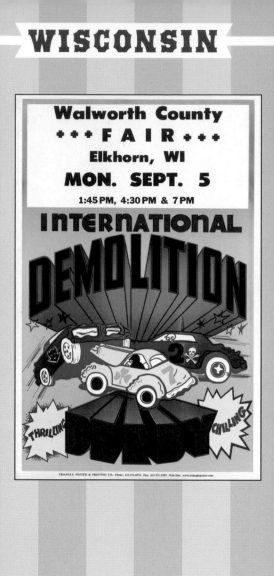

Walworth County
+++ **FAIR** +++
Elkhorn, WI
MON. SEPT. 5
1:45 PM, 4:30 PM & 7 PM

INTERNATIONAL
DEMOLITION
DERBY

THRILLING

CHILLING

WISCONSIN
STATE FAIR
MILWAUKEE
AUGUST
26, 27, 28, 29, 30, 31
(Over)

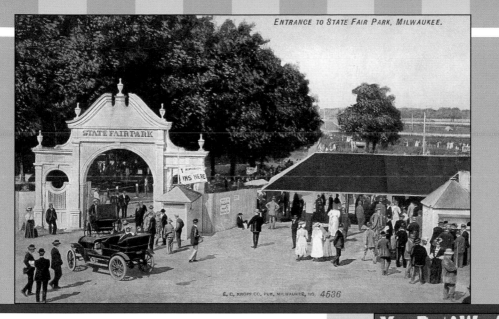

E. C. KROPP CO., PUB, MILWAUKEE, NO. 4536

Divide the oil between 2 large skillets with lids. Heat both over medium heat. Divide the garlic, onion, and bell peppers between the skillets and cook, stirring as needed, until the onion is translucent, about 5 minutes. Add the sausages, 4 to each skillet, and cook, turning several times, about 4 minutes longer, or until lightly browned on all sides. Add half of the tomatoes (½ cup), the wine (¾ cup), the oregano, and a pinch of salt to each pan. Cover, reduce the heat to medium-low, and simmer for about 25 minutes, or until the peppers are soft and the sausages are cooked through. Season with salt and pepper. Serve with crusty bread.

Serves 6 to 8

Coffee Cheesecake Pie with Coffee-Caramel Sauce

Ferne Freiberg of Casper, a cooking contest veteran, won the "Coffee with the *Casper Star-Tribune*" contest at the Central Wyoming Fair in Casper, and took home a blue ribbon as well as $100 in cash. The judges were especially impressed with the lightness of this dessert and its rich coffee flavor. Serve it with fresh or frozen raspberries for an extra-special treat. Held every mid-July since 1947, the fair combines a carnival, farm exhibitions, and rodeo competitions. Visitors can also watch tractor pulls, a demolition derby, and drill-team events.

Heat the oven to 350°F. Spray or lightly grease an 8-inch springform cake pan.

To make the crust: Combine the crumbs, sugar, and coffee granules in a small bowl and toss with a fork. Add the melted butter and toss again until the crumbs are evenly moistened. Gently press the mixture into the bottom of the pan. Sprinkle the nuts on top of the crust.

CRUST
½	cup Oreo cookie crumbs
1½	tablespoons sugar
¼	teaspoon instant coffee granules, any variety
2	tablespoons butter, melted
1	tablespoon finely ground walnuts

FILLING
One	8-ounce package cream cheese, softened
½	cup sugar
1	egg
2½	tablespoons plus ½ teaspoon brewed strong coffee

COFFEE-CARAMEL SAUCE
3	tablespoons caramel-flavored dessert topping (any variety)
¼	teaspoon instant coffee granules

To make the filling: Combine the cream cheese and sugar in a medium bowl and beat with an electric mixer until smooth. Add the egg and brewed coffee and mix well. Put the filling in the pan and bake for 25 minutes, or until the center is almost firm. Remove from the oven and place on a wire rack to cool completely.

To make the sauce: Combine the topping and coffee granules in a small saucepan and stir until smooth. Heat, stirring, over low heat to dissolve the coffee. Let cool and drizzle on the pie.

Variation: Melt 1 ounce of chocolate and drizzle it over the top of the pie in place of the coffee-caramel sauce.

Serves 4 to 6

How to Win a Blue Ribbon

Ready to try your hand at a winning recipe? Here are ten tips from blue-ribbon winners.

1. Visit your state or county fairs and look at the winning entries to figure out what sets them apart from the others.

2. Find out if the contest you are entering requires original recipes, or if you can use one straight out of a cookbook and simply give credit to your source.

3. Obtain a copy of the contest rules from the fair committee or the contest sponsor and read through them several times before you make anything. Pay attention to all the instructions. If they ask you to present your entry on a white paper plate, don't decide to use red. And if they require you to write down your recipe, put all the ingredients in the order that you use them, and be clear about the quantities and steps.

4. Come up with a special touch to set your recipe apart from all the others: a tomatillo dipping sauce for kebabs, a toasted-pecan topping for a peach pie, a strawberry filling for a pork roast.

5. Try to use unusual ingredients or combinations of ingredients (eggplant with cocoa powder, or a mix of herbs, nuts, seeds, and dried fruits).

6. Suggest preparing common ingredients in a new way: cutting vegetables on the diagonal, shredding them, stuffing them, roasting them.

7. Look for ways to make healthful food that tastes great by cutting back on fats and using vinegars, spices, and high temperatures to bring out flavor.

8. Give your recipe a good title to catch the judges' attention. Go for rhymes (Curry in a Hurry), alliteration (Peppery Poppy Seed Pretzels), or other word plays.

9. Be meticulous when assembling your entry. Don't leave any drips or spills on the rims of plates or bowls.

10. Don't be discouraged if you don't win a prize the first time you try. Keep entering, and talking with the winners to learn some of their secrets.

The Show Of Show Champions

Jr. Fair Sale Sept. 13 - 6:00 p.m.
HOCKING CO.
FAIR
Logan, Ohio

SEPT. 8-13

RECIPE PERMISSIONS

Alabama: Mary's Sticky Biscuits (page 12). Used by permission of Whitfield Foods.

Alaska: Melody's Molasses Crinkles (page 14). Used by permission of Joyce McCombs, "The Carefree Gourmet," The Delta News Web.

Arizona: Citrus Cowboy Creams (page 16). Used by permission of C&H Sugar Co.

Arkansas: Jackpot Cherry Pie (page 18). Used by permission of the Arkansas State Fair.

California: Salsa Jam (page 20). From *Blue Ribbon Preserves: Secrets to Award-Winning Jams, Jellies, Marmalades & More* by Linda J. Amendt (HP Books, 2001). Used by permission of Linda J. Amendt.

Colorado: Colorado Potato Cream Pie (page 22). Used by permission of the Colorado State Fair.

Connecticut: Country Fair "Caramel Apples" (page 24). Used by permission of the Association of Connecticut Fairs.

Delaware: Lakeshore Italian Steak and Potato Salad (page 26). Used by permission of the Delaware Beef and Potato Cook-Off and the Delaware Department of Agriculture.

Florida: Pecan Fudge Caramel Squares (page 28). Used by permission of *Florida Today*.

Georgia: Marie Antoinettes (page 30). Used by permission of the Georgia Egg Commission.

Hawaii: Blue Hawaiian (page 32). Used by permission of BlueCocktail.com.

Idaho: Sourdough Bread (page 34). Used by permission of Charles and Connie McGuffey.

Illinois: Soy Velvet Crumb Cake (page 36). Used by permission of the Illinois Soybean Association.

Indiana: Double-Chocolate Peanut Butter Chip Cookies (page 38). Used by permission of the Traditional Arts Indiana program.

Iowa: Cool Fruit Strata (page 40). Used by permission of the Iowa Heart Center.

Kansas: Strawberry Daisy Bread (page 42). Used by permission of Susan Krumm, County Extension Agent, Ashley Lesser, and the *Lawrence Journal-World*, Lawrence, Kansas.

Kentucky: Aunt Betsy's Bourbon Chowder with Onion-Pita Rounds (page 44). Used by permission of the Evan Williams Cooking Contest.

Louisiana: Pickled Okra (page 46). Used by permission of Alice Cormier.

Maine: New York–Style Half-Sour Pickles (page 48). Used by permission of Adam Tomash.

Maryland: Squash Pie (page 50). Used by permission of Frances Jaques, HometownAnnapolis.com/ Capital-Gazette Newspapers.

Massachusetts: Mini Raspberry Truffle Cakes (page 52). Used by permission of the Marshfield Fair.

Michigan: Pasties (page 54). Used by permission of the Upper Peninsula State Fair.

Minnesota: Marjorie Johnson's Sour Cream Streusel Coffee Cake (page 58). Used by permission of Marjorie Johnson.

Mississippi: Cajun Smothered Venison Steak (page 60). Used by permission of the South Mississippi Fair.

Missouri: Catfish Wraps (page 62). Used by permission of the Missouri Conservation Agents Association.

Montana: Beef Roll-Ups (page 66). Used by permission of the Montana Beef Cookoff, sponsored by Montana Cattlewomen.

Nebraska: Creamy Cheesecake (page 68). Used by permission of the Nebraska State Fair.

Nevada: Grilled Salsa (page 70). Used by permission of the Nevada State Fair.

New Hampshire: Rosy Spiced Crab Apples (page 72). Used by permission of Cynthia Van Hazinga.

New Jersey: Apple-Carrot Muffins (page 74). Used by permission of the Warren County Farmers' Fair.

New Mexico: Korean Oven-Roasted Turkey SPAM Stir-Fry (page 76). Used by permission of the Hormel Foods Corporation.

New York: Governor Davis Apple Pie (page 78). Used by permission of the New York State Fair.

North Carolina: Roasted Chicken Salad with Honey-Pecan Balsamic Dressing (page 82). Used by permission of the North Carolina Pecan Association.

North Dakota: Susan's Fettuccine (page 84). Used by permission of Susan Sorvaag.

Ohio: Don's Peach Pie (page 86). Used by permission of Carol Michael.

Oklahoma: Oklahoma Wagon Wheels (page 88). Used by permission of *The Oklahoman*. Copyright 2005, The Oklahoma Publishing Company.

Oregon: Bacon Cheeseburger Potato Salad (page 90). Used by permission of the Oregon Potato Commission.

Pennsylvania: Jim Bob's Chocolate-Molasses Cake (page 92). Used by permission of the Pennsylvania Farm Show.

Rhode Island: Apple-Cinnamon Oatmeal Bread (page 94). Used by permission of the Washington County Fair.

South Carolina: Japanese Fruitcake (page 96). From *Ribbon-Winning Recipes: South Carolina State Fair.* Used by permission of the South Carolina State Fair.

South Dakota: Pumpkin Streusel Sweet Rolls (page 98). Used by permission of Jill Callison, *Sioux Falls Argus Leader.*

Tennessee: Strawberry Cobbler (page 100). Used by permission of Connie Cobern.

Texas: Mushroom Moussaka (page 102). From the *2005 State Fair of Texas Prize-Winning Recipes Cookbook.* Used by permission of the State Fair of Texas.

Utah: Five-Minute Crock-Pot Burritos (page 106). Used by permission of the *Deseret Morning News.*

Vermont: Vegetarian Stuffed-Pepper Medley (page 108). Used by permission of the Cabot Creamery.

Virginia: Championship Chili (page 110). Used by permission of John T. Maxwell.

Washington: Chocolate Crunch Brownies (page 112). Used by permission of Darice J. Oliver.

West Virginia: Marbled Banana Bars (page 114). Used by permission of Land O'Lakes, Inc.

Wisconsin: Old-Fashioned Sausages and Peppers (page 116). Used by permission of Usinger's, courtesy of the *Milwaukee Journal Sentinel.*

Wyoming: Coffee Cheesecake Pie with Coffee-Caramel Sauce (page 120). Used by permission of Sally Ann Shurmur, *Casper Star-Tribune.*

ILLUSTRATION CREDITS

Cover: West Alabama State Fair, Tuscaloosa, Alabama, poster detail, courtesy of Triangle Poster Company, Pittsburgh, PA.

2. (clockwise from right) Program cover, 1949; Danbury, CT Speedway ticket, 1980; Nebraska State Fair ticket stub.

3. (left) County Fair pass, 1909; (right) Handbill, 1930.

6. State Fair program cover, 1961.

7. State Fair program cover, 1958.

8. Los Angeles County Fair brochure, 1941.

9. Inter State Fair program cover, 1948.

10. State Fair sticker, ca. 1910.

11. (clockwise from left) Indiana county fair program cover, 1952; Ohio county fair program cover, 1948; Good luck card, 1910.

13. (left) Sticker, 1912, Nick Follansbee Collection; (right) Poster, courtesy of Triangle Poster Company, Pittsburgh, PA.

15. (clockwise from right) Brochure, ca. 1950; Poster stamp, Nick Follansbee Collection; Two "covers," 1977.

17. (left) State Fair brochure cover, 1958; (right) State Fair program cover, 2005.

18. Sticker.

19. (left and right) Postcards, ca. 1915 and 1909.

21. (clockwise from top left) Sticker, 1941; Brochure cover, 1940; Sticker, 1938.

23. State Fair program covers, 1961 and 1950.

25. (clockwise from left) Die-cut menu, Red Apple Inn, Carlsbad-by-the-Sea, CA, ca. 1930; Large letter postcard, ca. 1960; Linen postcard, ca. 1940.

27. (clockwise from left) Postcard, 1914; Mobilgas postcard, ca. 1950; Large letter postcard, ca. 1943.

29. State Fair brochure cover, 1951.

31. (left) Egg carton art, ca. 1950; Travel booklet cover, 1930.

32. Travel pamphlet, 1946.

33. Brochure cover, 1929.

34. Sticker, 1910, Nick Follansbee Collection.

35. (left) Poster, courtesy of Triangle Poster Company, Pittsburgh, PA; Travel brochure cover, ca. 1965.

37. (left) Program cover, 1955; (right) Race program, 1955.

39. (left) Program cover, 1946; Poster, courtesy of Triangle Poster Company, Pittsburgh, PA.

40. Large letter postcard, ca.1940.

41. (clockwise from left) Die-cut sticker, ca. 1940, and front cover flap image; Program cover, 1952; Blotter, 1939.

43. (from left) Postcard, 1911, Hal Ottaway Collection; Trade card, 1883; Sticker, ca. 1950.

45. (from left) Butter cow exhibit postcard, 1932; Horse show program, 1948.

47. (from left) Poster, courtesy of Triangle Poster Company, Pittsburgh, PA; Travel brochure cover, ca. 1950.

49. (clockwise from left) Premium list cover, 1928; Trade card, 1896; Postcard, ca. 1920.

51. (from left) Nebraska State Fair program cover, 1951; Travel brochure cover, 1932.

53. (from left) Program cover, 1948; Program cover, 1913.

55: Program cover, 1928, courtesy of First Upper Peninsula State Fair, Escanaba, Michigan.

56: State Fair program cover, 1988.

57. (from left) State Fair program cover, 1951; Premium list cover, 1927.

59. (from left) Butter sculpture blotter, 1925; Handbill, ca. 1943.

61. (from top left) Minnesota State Fair Grounds postcard, ca. 1910; Cardboard posters, undated, courtesy of Triangle Poster Company, Pittsburgh, PA.

63. (left and right) State Fair program cover and State Fair brochure, 1953.

64. (from left) Brochure cover, 1953; Program cover, 1961.

65. Program cover, Leland and Crystal Payton Collection.

66. Real photo postcard, ca. 1935.

67. (clockwise from left) County Fair program cover, 1961; Poster stamp, ca. 1910; State Fair brochure cover, 1940.

68. Poster stamp, 1936.

69. (from left) Program covers, 1959 and 1958.

71. (clockwise from top) Bumper sticker, ca. 1990s; Blue ribbon, 1945; Travel brochure cover, ca. 1945; Travel brochure cover, ca. 1950.

73. (from left) State Fair program cover, 1962; Travel brochure cover, ca. 1950.

75. (from top) Race program cover, 1959; Postcard, ca. 1915.

77. (left) Two poster stamps, 1915; New Mexico State Fairgrounds, Albuquerque, Photograph ©1987 John Margolies/Esto.

79. (left) Three postcards, 1909; State Fair program cover, 1906.

80. (clockwise from left) Die-cut coaster, 1938; Leather postcard, ca. 1910; Postcard, ca. 1915.

81. Postcard, ca. 1910.

83. (clockwise from left) Die-cut poster stamp, ca. 1930; State Fair program cover, 1953; Stuckey's booklet cover, ca. 1950.

85. (from left) Premium list cover, 1963; Travel brochure cover, ca. 1950.

87. (clockwise from top left) Student ticket, 1941; State Fair program cover, 1946; Music program cover, 1948.

89. (top) Decorated envelope, 1924; State Fair program cover, 1965.

91. (clockwise from top left) Salem County Fair photograph, 1909; Postcard, 1911; Champion bull real photo postcard, ca. 1910.

93. (clockwise from left) Postcard, ca. 1910; Poster stamp, 1916; Sticker, ca. 1922.

95: (from left) Book cover, 1922; Travel brochure cover, 1937.

97. Sticker, 1915, Nick Follansbee Collection; Travel brochure cover, ca. 1910.

99. (from left) Postcard, ca. 1910; State Fair program cover, 1908.

101. (clockwise from left) State Fair program covers, 1952 and 1954; First day cover, 1957.

103. State Fair program cover and back cover, 1947.

104. (from left) Big Tex at State Fairgrounds postcard, ca. 1960; State Fair program cover, 1941.

105. Trade card, 1892.

107. (clockwise from top left) Die-cut sticker, ca. 1940; Season pass, 1927; Golden Spike National Livestock Show Building photograph, Ogden, UT, ©1980 John Margolies, 1980/Esto.

109. (left) First day cover, 1989; Postcard, ca. 1910.

111. (from left) Poster courtesy of Triangle Poster Company, Pittsburgh, PA; Brochure cover, 1952; Stable pass, 1906.

113. State Fair program cover, 1975.

115. (clockwise from left) Poster, courtesy of Triangle Poster Company, Pittsburgh, PA; Postcard, ca. 1920; Postcard, ca. 1915.

116. Felt pennant, ca. 1950.

117. State Fair program cover, 1936.

118. (from left) Poster, courtesy of Triangle Poster Company, Pittsburgh, PA; Handbill, 1929, Nick Follansbee Collection.

119. (top) Postcard, ca. 1910; Poster stamp, 1916, Nick Follansbee Collection.

121. (from left) Travel brochure cover, ca. 1950; State Fair program cover, 1905.

123. Cardboard tabletop sign-poster, ca. 1950.

Back cover: (clockwise from left) Maine State Fair trade card, 1894; Delaware County, Indiana, fair program; Oklahoma State Fair decorated envelope, 1924.

INDEX

Apples
  Apple-Carrot Muffins, 74–75
  Apple-Cinnamon Oatmeal Bread, 94
  Governor Davis Apple Pie, 78, 81
  Rosy Spiced Crab Apples, 72

Bacon Cheeseburger Potato Salad, 90–91
Banana Bars, Marbled, 114–15
Beef
  Bacon Cheeseburger Potato Salad, 90–91
  Beef Roll-ups, 66–67
  Championship Chili, 110–11
  Lakeshore Italian Steak and Potato Salad, 26–27
  Pasties, 54, 57
Beverages
  Blue Hawaiian, 32
Biscuits, Mary's Sticky, 12–13
Bread
  Apple-Cinnamon Oatmeal Bread, 94
  Sourdough Bread, 34–35
  Strawberry Daisy Bread, 42–43
Brownies, Chocolate Crunch, 112
Burritos, Five-Minute Crock-Pot, 106

Cakes
  Creamy Cheesecake, 68–69
  Japanese Fruitcake, 96–97
  Jim Bob's Chocolate-Molasses Cake, 92–93
  Marjorie Johnson's Sour Cream Streusel Coffee Cake, 58–59
  Mini Raspberry Truffle Cakes, 52
  Soy Velvet Crumb Cake, 36–37
Candies
  Citrus Cowboy Creams, 16–17
  Pecan Fudge Caramel Squares, 28
Catfish Wraps, 62, 65
Cheesecakes
  Coffee Cheesecake Pie with Coffee-Caramel Sauce, 120–21
  Creamy Cheesecake, 68–69
Cherry Pie, Jackpot, 18–19
Chicken Salad, Roasted, with Honey-Pecan Balsamic Dressing, 82–83
Chocolate
  Chocolate Crunch Brownies, 112
  Citrus Cowboy Creams, 16–17

Double-Chocolate Peanut Butter Chip Cookies, 38–39
Jim Bob's Chocolate-Molasses Cake, 92–93
Marbled Banana Bars, 114–15
Mini Raspberry Truffle Cakes, 52
Pecan Fudge Caramel Squares, 28
Chowder, Aunt Betsy's Bourbon, 44–45
Cobbler, Strawberry, 100–101
Coffee Cheesecake Pie with Coffee-Caramel Sauce, 120–21
Cookies
  Double-Chocolate Peanut Butter Chip Cookies, 38–39
  Melody's Molasses Crinkles, 14

Fruit. See also individual fruits
  Cool Fruit Strata, 40–41
  Japanese Fruitcake, 96–97

Jam, Salsa, 20–21

Marie Antoinettes, 30–31
Moussaka, Mushroom, 102, 105
Muffins
  Apple-Carrot Muffins, 74–75
  Country Fair "Caramel Apples," 24–25

Okra, Pickled, 46
Onion-Pita Rounds, 44–45

Pasta
  Susan's Fettuccine, 84
Pasties, 54, 57
Pastries
  Marie Antoinettes, 30–31
Peach Pie, Don's, 86
Pecan Fudge Caramel Squares, 28
Peppers
  Old-Fashioned Sausages and Peppers, 116, 119
  Vegetarian Stuffed-Pepper Medley, 108–9
Pickles
  New York–Style Half-Sour Pickles, 48–49
  Pickled Okra, 46
Pies
  Coffee Cheesecake Pie with Coffee-Caramel Sauce, 120–21

Colorado Potato Cream Pie, 22–23
Don's Peach Pie, 86
Governor Davis Apple Pie, 78, 81
Jackpot Cherry Pie, 18–19
Squash Pie, 50
Pork
  Championship Chili, 110–11
  Five-Minute Crock-Pot Burritos, 106
  Pasties, 54, 57
Potatoes
  Bacon Cheeseburger Potato Salad, 90–91
  Colorado Potato Cream Pie, 22–23
  Lakeshore Italian Steak and Potato Salad, 26–27
Pumpkin Streusel Sweet Rolls, 98–99

Raspberry Truffle Cakes, Mini, 52
Rolls
  Oklahoma Wagon Wheels, 88–89
  Pumpkin Streusel Sweet Rolls, 98–99

Salads
  Bacon Cheeseburger Potato Salad, 90–91
  Lakeshore Italian Steak and Potato Salad, 26–27
  Roasted Chicken Salad with Honey-Pecan Balsamic Dressing, 82–83
Salsa, Grilled, 70
Salsa Jam, 20–21
Sausages and Peppers, Old-Fashioned, 116, 119
Seafood
  Aunt Betsy's Bourbon Chowder with Onion-Pita Rounds, 44–45
  Catfish Wraps, 62, 65
SPAM Stir-Fry, Korean Oven-Roasted Turkey, 76–77
Squash Pie, 50
Strawberries
  Marie Antoinettes, 30–31
  Strawberry Cobbler, 100–101
  Strawberry Daisy Bread, 42–43

Tomatoes
  Grilled Salsa, 70
  Salsa Jam, 20–21

Venison Steak, Cajun Smothered, 60

TABLE OF EQUIVALENTS

The exact equivalents in the following table have been rounded for convenience.

LIQUID/DRY MEASURES

U.S.	METRIC
¼ teaspoon	1.25 milliliters
½ teaspoon	2.5 milliliters
1 teaspoon	5 milliliters
1 tablespoon (3 teaspoons)	15 milliliters
1 fluid ounce (2 tablespoons)	30 milliliters
¼ cup	60 milliliters
⅓ cup	80 milliliters
½ cup	120 milliliters
1 cup	240 milliliters
1 pint (2 cups)	480 milliliters
1 quart (4 cups; 32 ounces)	960 milliliters
1 gallon (4 quarts)	3.84 liters
1 ounce (by weight)	28 grams
1 pound	448 grams
2.2 pounds	1 kilogram

LENGTHS

U.S.	METRIC
⅛ inch	3 millimeters
¼ inch	6 millimeters
½ inch	12 millimeters
1 inch	2.5 centimeters

OVEN TEMPERATURES

FAHRENHEIT	CELSIUS	GAS
250	120	½
275	140	1
300	150	2
325	160	3
350	180	4
375	190	5
400	200	6
425	220	7
450	230	8
475	240	9
500	260	10